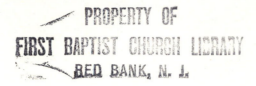
"... NOT I, BUT CHRIST ..."

Galatians 2:20

Basic Lesson Series—Volume 4

NOT I BUT CHRIST

"Exercise thyself unto godliness"
1 Timothy 4:7

WATCHMAN NEE

Christian Fellowship Publishers, Inc.
New York

Available from the Publishers at:

11515 Allecingie Parkway
Richmond, Virginia 23235

PRINTED IN U.S.A.

Basic Lessons—Volume 4

CONTENTS

BASIC LESSONS
ON
PRACTICAL CHRISTIAN LIVING

Burdened with the need of a firm foundation for the Christian life, brother Watchman Nee gave a series of basic lessons on practical Christian living during the training session for workers held in Kuling, Foochow, China in 1948. He expressed the hope that these essential lessons might be faithfully learned by God's people, thereby laying a good foundation for the building up of the Body of Christ.

These messages on practical Christian living have now been translated from the Chinese language and will be published in a series of six books, bearing the various titles of: (1) *A Living Sacrifice*; (2) *The Good Confession*; (3) *Assembling Together*; (4) *Not I, But Christ*; (5) *Do All to the Glory of God*; and (6) *Love One Another*.

"Exercise thyself unto godliness" (1 Tim. 4:7), is the exhortation of the apostle Paul. May our hearts be so exercised by God's Word as to give the Holy Spirit opportunity to perfect the new creation.

All quotations of the Scriptures, unless otherwise indicated, are from the American Standard Version of the Bible (1901).

IF ANY MAN SIN

And Jehovah spake unto Moses and unto Aaron, saying, This is the statute of the law which Jehovah hath commanded, saying, Speak unto the children of Israel, that they bring thee a red heifer without spot, wherein is no blemish, and upon which never came yoke. And ye shall give her unto Eleazar the priest, and he shall bring her forth without the camp, and one shall slay her before his face: and Eleazar the priest shall take of her blood with his finger, and sprinkle of her blood toward the front of the tent of meeting seven times. And one shall burn the heifer in his sight; her skin, and her flesh, and her blood, with her dung, shall he burn: and the priest shall take cedar-wood, and hyssop, and scarlet, and cast it into the midst of the burning of the heifer. Then the priest shall wash his clothes, and he shall bathe his flesh in water, and afterward he shall come into the camp, and the priest shall be unclean until the even. And he that burneth her shall wash his clothes in water, and bathe his flesh in water, and shall be unclean until the even. And a man that is clean shall gather up the ashes of the heifer, and lay them up without the camp in a clean place; and it shall be kept for the congregation of the children of Israel for a water for

1

impurity: it is a sin-offering. And he that gathereth the ashes of the heifer shall wash his clothes, and be unclean until the even: and it shall be unto the children of Israel, and unto the stranger that sojourneth among them, for a statute for ever. . . . the same shall purify himself therewith on the third day, and on the seventh day he shall be clean: but if he purify not himself the third day, then the seventh day he shall not be clean. Whosoever toucheth a dead person, the body of a man that hath died, and purifieth not himself, defileth the tabernacle of Jehovah; and that soul shall be cut off from Israel: because the water for impurity was not sprinkled upon him, he shall be unclean; his uncleanness is yet upon him. . . . And for the unclean they shall take of the ashes of the burning of the sin-offering; and running water shall be put thereto in a vessel: and a clean person shall take hyssop, and dip it in the water, and sprinkle it upon the tent, and upon all the vessels, and upon the persons that were there, and upon him that touched the bone, or the slain, or the dead, or the grave: and the clean person shall sprinkle upon the unclean on the third day, and on the seventh day: and on the seventh day he shall purify him; and he shall wash his clothes, and bathe himself in water, and shall be clean at even.

Num. 19:1–10, 12–13, 17–19

But if we walk in the light, as he is in the light, we have fellowship one with another, and the blood of Jesus his Son cleanseth us from all sin. If we say that we have no sin, we deceive ourselves, and the truth is not in us. If we confess our sins, he is faithful and righteous to forgive us our sins, and to cleanse us from all unrighteousness. If we say that we have not sinned, we make him a liar, and his word is not in us. My little children, these things write I unto you that ye may not sin. And if any man sin, we have an Advocate with the Father, Jesus Christ the righteous: and he is the propitiation for our sins; and not for ours only, but also for the whole world.

1 John 1:7–2:2

The Redemption of the Cross and the Work of the Holy Spirit

If a redeemed person should inadvertently sin, how can he be restored to God? This is a very pressing problem. Unless he knows the way of restoration, he will not be able to come back to God.

1. THE LORD'S WORK AND THE HOLY SPIRIT'S WORK CONTRASTED

By His death on the cross, the Lord Jesus cleansed and redeemed us from all our sins. At the time we came to Him, the Holy Spirit enlightened us and showed us our sins. But what the Holy Spirit showed us was not as comprehensive as what the Lord did on the cross. The difference is worth noticing. Even as the sin-offering in Leviticus 16 included every sin, so also the Lord Jesus on the cross bore all of our sins. His redemption covered every sin that you could possibly commit in your lifetime. Indeed, when He died on the cross, He bore all the sins of your life.

However, when the Holy Spirit inspires us to believe in the Lord, He can only move us to repent of our past sins, not of all the sins of our life. The Holy Spirit's conviction is based on the sins we have already committed, not the sins we have not yet committed! Therefore, on the day we are saved, we are convicted by the light of the Holy Spirit of far fewer sins than those our Lord bore on the cross for us. What the Lord Jesus dealt with on the cross is entirely inclusive; but what I am convicted of by the Holy Spirit and receive forgiveness for, refers only to those sins which I have committed up to the day that I first trust in the Lord.

The Holy Spirit never tries to convict me of sins which I have not committed. I have no knowledge of them nor feeling of guilt. Hence there is a difference between the Lord Jesus bearing our sins and the Holy Spirit convicting us of our sins. This is what the apostle John tries to make us understand.

2. BASIS FOR KNOWING THE LORD'S GRACE

All sins of the past, all those committed before the day of our salvation no matter what our age at that time, are assuredly forgiven. But we should know that the sins forgiven us then are fewer than the sins which the Lord has actually borne for us. We know the Lord's grace only according to our personal experience of sinning. The Lord, however, has borne all our sins according to His full knowledge of us—that is, all the sins which we will ever commit.

Sinning after Being Saved

One who has been saved and who afterward sinned again may be greatly distressed by it. Since I started to serve God's people in 1921, I have been asked by many about this problem of sinning after being saved. They say: I know the Lord has forgiven all my sins, that I am already saved and totally forgiven. But since I have been saved, I have again committed many sins. I am deeply troubled by these sins. What can I do about them?

1. WHAT THE LORD BORE ON THE CROSS

I hope you have understood that all the sins which you may commit after you are saved are included in the redemption of the Lord Jesus—even though you do not *feel* forgiven.

Suppose a young brother is saved at the age of sixteen and also suppose that up to that sixteenth year, he has committed a thousand sins. Proportionally, by the time he is thirty-two, he will have doubled his sins—that is, he will have committed two thousand. But when he trusted in the Lord at the age of sixteen, he undoubtedly prayed, "Lord, I thank You, for You have forgiven all my sins. You have borne them all on the cross." Doesn't this mean that every one of his one thousand sins is forgiven? Now suppose that instead of being saved at sixteen, he is saved at thirty-two. What would he say to the Lord at that time? Would it not be the same prayer, "Lord, You have borne all my sins away"? We may further speculate that if he is saved at sixty-four, he will still pray the same way, "Lord, You have borne all my sins." It is therefore evident that at whatever age one is saved, he is assured that the Lord bears all his sins.

2. DIFFERENCES IN EXPERIENCE

If you are saved at sixteen, the Lord certainly has borne all your sins from your birth to sixteen years of age. But know also that He has borne all your sins from sixteen till sixty-four as well. Whether you are saved earlier or later has no relation to the Lord's bearing away your sins. For this reason, do not be so foolish as to question what the Lord can do about your sins after salvation. Were you to be saved a few years later, would it be possible that He would not bear your sins? No, the Lord has borne all your sins on the cross. The robber on the cross believed on the Lord with his last breath, but he had all his sins borne by the Lord. In other words, the Lord has actually borne the sins of our whole life, even though at the time of salvation we only experience the forgiveness of those sins which we have committed in the past.

How to Return to God after Sinning

We have no intention to encourage young brothers and sisters to live a loose life. In another lesson we will point out to them the way of victory (Lesson 26, "Deliverance"). Our purpose for this lesson is to show how one who has sinned can be restored to God.

1. OLD TESTAMENT TYPE

We will now look at an Old Testament type that illustrates restoration to God after one has sinned.

THE UNIQUE OFFERING OF THE RED HEIFER

Numbers 19 is a most unusual chapter in the Old Testament. All the offerings in the Bible are bullocks and rams, but here there is an exception—a heifer, a female cow. All the offerings in the Old Testament are slaughtered and offered to God, but this offering of the red heifer, though killed and burned, is very different from the rest. While all others are offered to God to meet current claims—that is, the sin-offering, the burnt-offering, or the peace-offering according to the need of the day—the red heifer alone was not for the present need. It was offered to meet future needs. This is something for young brethren to remember.

Through Moses and Aaron the Lord commanded the people to bring a red heifer to Him. Notice that it was not a bullock but a heifer. Sex has its significance in the Bible. All that pertains to truth and testimony is represented by the male sex, while all that speaks of experience and life is symbolized by the female sex. This is a principle in the study of the Bible. Abraham represents justification by faith, and Sarah stands for obedience. Faith is objective, truthful, a testimony; obedience is subjective and experiental. The church as seen in the Bible is always referred to by the feminine pronoun because she represents the subjective work of the Lord upon men. The work of the red heifer is therefore subjective, not objective, in nature.

THE BLOOD OF THE RED HEIFER

What had to be done to the red heifer? After it was slain, its blood was to be sprinkled toward the front of the tent of meeting seven times. This was to indicate that the blood was offered to God. The blood always works Godward. If it is not for God, it is useless. Today we are redeemed because God has remitted our sins. To sprinkle the blood of the red heifer toward the tent of meeting seven times was to offer it to God. In this respect, this offering is joined to the other offerings. As the other offerings are to atone for sins before God, so this offering is for the atonement of sins.

THE BURNING OF THE RED HEIFER

Here we find the special feature of the red heifer. "And one shall burn the heifer in his sight; her skin, and her flesh, and her blood, with her dung, shall he burn" (v. 5). The whole heifer was to be burned; not a single bit remained unconsumed. "And the priest shall take cedarwood, and hyssop, and scarlet, and cast it into the midst of the burning of the heifer" (v. 6). The cedar and hyssop represent the world, the entire universe. In describing the wisdom of Solomon, it is said that, "he spake of trees, from the cedar that is in Lebanon even unto the hyssop that springeth out of the wall" (1 Kings 4:33a). So, figuratively, the whole world was burned with the red heifer. The scarlet, I think, represents our sins, as we find in Isaiah, "though your sins be as scarlet" (1:18). In other words, the sins of the whole world were consumed with this heifer which was offered to God.

In this type we find the cross portrayed. When the Lord Jesus offered Himself to God, He took with Him to the cross all our sins, the sins of the whole world. Great sins and small sins, sins of yesterday, sins of today, and sins of tomorrow are all included. Even sins which humanly may be reckoned as unforgiveable are a part of the offering. All sins were heaped on the red heifer and were consumed with it.

THE ASHES OF THE RED HEIFER

After the burning, then what? "And a man that is clean shall gather up the ashes of the heifer, and lay them up without the camp in a clean place; and it shall be kept for the congregation of the children of Israel for a water for impurity: it is a sin-offering" (v. 9). What is meant by "for a water for impurity"? Here lies the uniqueness of the red heifer. Unlike other offerings, which had only their blood sprinkled before God, the ashes of the red heifer were kept for future use. Its efficacy was in the blood. The ashes which were collected from the burning of the red heifer together with the cedar and hyssop and scarlet were stored in a clean place. What was the purpose? It was that one day when an Israelite sinned by touching something unclean, he might then go to the priest who would mix the ashes with running water and sprinkle them upon the

8

unclean person to make him clean. In other words, the ashes were used to take away defilement and sin.

According to the Old Testament, an offering was required for every sin. But here it is different. Here is a man who has already presented his offering and then later on has touched something unclean. Because he has been defiled, he cannot have fellowship with God. What should he do? He should go to the priest for the water for impurity that his defilement may be cleansed and his sin forgiven. This is quite a different type from the other offerings. The ashes of the burned heifer were kept for the cleansing of the many defilements of future days.

Bullocks were offered by people who were conscious of their sins. If I were an Israelite, I could bring a bullock or a sheep to God and offer it as a sin-offering because I was aware of my many sins. But the offering of the red heifer was different. It was burned not for the sake of my past known sins but rather to prepare for future cleansings. In this we see another aspect of the redemptive work of the Lord Jesus, quite different from that of which the bullocks and sheep in the Old Testament speak.

New believers ought to know this aspect of the Lord's work, the aspect typified by the ashes of the red heifer. All the efficacy of redemption is embodied in the ashes, all the sins of the world are included. The blood was in these ashes. At any time thereafter, whenever one was defiled through touching an unclean thing, he had no need to slay another red heifer; he only needed to be sprinkled with the water for impurity containing the ashes of a red heifer. In other words, a believer today does not need the Lord to work for him a second time, since there is already provision for the cleansing of all his future defilements in our Lord's work of redemption. The Lord has already made full provision.

THE SCRIPTURAL MEANING OF THE ASHES

Perhaps some will ask what the ashes signify. Why must the red heifer be burned to ashes? Why should these ashes be collected?

The answer is that in the Bible ashes are used as a basic unit of matter. Ashes in the Bible are the last form of all things. Whether it be a cow or a horse or whatever it may be, it becomes ash when it is reduced to its final form. Ashes, therefore, are the final, irreducible unit. They are not only unchangeable but also incorruptible. They are not subject to rust or decay. They are most enduring. They are ultimate.

The redemptive work of the Lord as typified by the burning of the red heifer to ashes reveals a condition which is permanent and unchanged. What the Lord has done for us in His work of redemption can never be changed. It is most constant. Do not think the rocks on the mountain are enduring, for these can still be burned to ashes. Ashes, being the final form of all matter, are more constant than rocks. Likewise, the redemption which the Lord has provided for us is unchangeable, undefileable, and incorruptible. It is available to us at all times. The flesh, the skin, and the blood of the heifer are subject to corruption, but when they become ashes, they are beyond corruption. Our redemption is, therefore, eternally efficacious. Whenever we touch an unclean thing and are defiled, we need not ask the Lord to die once more for us. We have the incorruptible ashes and we have the living water of life. We know the ashes are ever effectual in cleansing us.

To put it another way: the ashes of the red heifer

represent the finished work of the cross for today's use as well as for future need. We declare that the red heifer, once burned to ashes, is sufficient for all the needs of our lifetime. We thank God for the all-sufficiency of the redemption of the Lord Jesus. We come to see more and more that His death does indeed atone for all our sins.

2. WALK IN THE LIGHT

"But if we walk in the light, as he is in the light, we have fellowship with one another, and the blood of Jesus his Son cleanseth us from all sin" (1 John 1:7). What does the "light" here refer to? It has two possible meanings: one possibility is the light of holiness; the other possibility is the light of the gospel, that is, God revealed and manifested in the gospel.

Many would like the "light" here to refer to the light of holiness. Thus the first section of this verse might be paraphrased thus: "if we walk in holiness as God is in holiness." Such a rendering, however, would make what follows meaningless. It is quite evident that we have no need of the blood of Jesus, God's Son, to cleanse us from our sins if we are holy.

God has distinctly declared that He comes to save us and give us grace. If we are in this light as God is in the light of grace, the light of the gospel, then we can have fellowship one with another. By grace we come to God as He also comes to us in grace. Thus we have fellowship with God, and the blood of Jesus His Son cleanses us from all our sins. This truly is grace.

Once Mr. J. N. Darby was conducting a meeting in the northern part of the United States. A good man in the Methodist Church by the name of Mr. Daniel Steele admired him very much. These two men, however, did not see eye to eye. Darby very much stressed the grace of God, while Steele emphasized God's way in us. Though their ways differed, yet Mr. Steele always went to hear Mr. Darby. On one occasion, Darby spoke on 1 John 1:7, interpreting it as the principle of the gospel—"If we walk in the light of the gospel as God is in the light of the gospel." Formerly we did not know God, the God who reveals Himself in the gospel; now we know Him by the revelation of the gospel, for God has revealed Himself in this light of His grace. Having come to God in the light of the grace of His gospel, we now have fellowship with God.

At this point Mr. Steele could stand it no longer, for such teaching smashed his Wesleyan doctrine to pieces. So he stood up and challenged, "But brother Darby, suppose a real Christian turns his back on the light, what then?" "Then the light will shine on his back," answered Mr. Darby. Mr. Darby spoke many wonderful words during his life, but I think this was one of the best. In Mr. Steele's eye, it was beyond hope if anyone resisted the holy light of God. Knowing him well, Mr. Darby simply replied, "Then the light will shine on his back."

Later on, another Methodist by the name of Mr. Griffith Thomas acknowledged that the light here should be the light of the gospel, for God has revealed Himself fully in the gospel. Today we have fellowship with the God who is revealed to us in the gospel; the result is that the blood of Jesus His Son cleanses us from all our sins. This cleansing is conditional on our walking in the light.

We hope new believers will see that God is the God who reveals Himself. He no longer hides Himself in darkness as He did in the time of the Old Testament. Today God can be known and seen. The Athenians worshiped an unknown god, unknowable as well as unknown, who hid himself in darkness. But today, through the gospel, God has come forth. He is in the light, and by that light we may see Him. We know Him as God because He has revealed Himself. We have fellowship with Him in His light; consequently the blood of Jesus His Son cleanses all our sins.

3. CONFESSION AND THE GRACE OF FORGIVENESS

"If we say that we have no sin, we deceive ourselves, and the truth is not in us" (1 John 1:8). We deceive ourselves if we say we have no sin. It is evident that the truth is not in us. This is certain.

"If we confess our sins, he is faithful and righteous to forgive us our sins, and to cleanse us from all unrighteousness" (v. 9). If we know we have sinned and also confess it, God will forgive our sins and cleanse us from all unrighteousness. He is faithful to His own Word and righteous toward His own work, faithful to His own promise and righteous toward the redemptive work of His Son on the cross. He cannot but forgive for He has said it; He must forgive because of the work of redemption. Due to His faithfulness and righteousness, He will forgive us our sins and cleanse us from all unrighteousness.

"If we say that we have not sinned, we make him a liar, and his word is not in us" (v. 10). How can we say we have never sinned? That would make God a liar and would refute the necessity for redemption. God provides us with redemption because we have sinned.

"My little children, these things write I unto you that ye may not sin. And if any man sin, we have an Advocate with the Father, Jesus Christ the righteous" (1 John 2:1). "These things" refers back to the words in chapter 1:7–10; there God depicts in principle our various conditions

13

before Him due to our sins. Because of the blood of Jesus His Son, God forgives us our sins. Owing to His faithfulness and righteousness, He forgives and cleanses all our unrighteousness. No matter what kinds of sins we have committed, they all are forgiven.

What the Lord has done is to wholly forgive and totally cleanse us from all our sins and all our unrighteousness. When He says "all," no doubt He *means* "all." Do not change His Word. He forgives not only our sins of the past but all of our sins—sins that we are conscious of as well as those of which we are unaware. We go away with a perfect and complete forgiveness.

"These things," therefore, alludes to how our sins are forgiven through the promise and work of God. God has spoken to us that we may not sin. When we see the Lord's great forgiveness to us, far from becoming careless, we rather are constrained not to sin.

What follows is something quite specific. The sins already mentioned are more general in nature and the forgiveness experienced is also general in principle. But what about the sins committed after we have believed in the Lord? What specific forgiveness is there? "And if any man sin"—this refers to a child of God—"we have an Advocate with the Father, Jesus Christ the righteous." "With the Father" shows that it is a family affair. We are counted among the children of God; we belong to the family. We have an advocate with the Father, even Jesus Christ the righteous, who is the propitiation for our sins. Because He became the propitiation for our sins in His death, He is now our advocate with the Father.

If a Christian should sin, he has an advocate with the Father. There is a Father-son relationship if the one who sins is a believer. The word *advocate* in the Greek is *parakletos* which means "called to one's side." It has two different usages: in civil use it means one who stands by and is ever ready to help; in legal use it means a counselor or attorney, one who takes full responsibility for the case. Our Lord took us in when we first came to His cross. How did He assume our case? By being "the propitiation for our sins and not for ours only, but also for the whole world" (1 John 2:2).

Propitiation here is comparable to the ashes of the red heifer in Numbers 19. As we have mentioned, the provision found in Numbers 19 is for future use. Likewise, forgiveness of our sins, including those of the present and future, is based on the finished work of the cross. There is no need for a new cross, for the redemptive work of the cross is eternally efficacious.

New believers should clearly be exhorted not to sin. They ought not to sin and it is actually possible for them not to sin. But if they should unfortunately sin, let them remember that the blood of the Lord Jesus can still cleanse them from all their sins. He is their champion; He is the righteous One. The very fact that He is now with the Father guarantees the forgiveness of their sins.

Since this is so, do not linger in the shame of sin as if such suffering will bring in holiness. Do not think that to prolong the consciousness of sin is in any way an indication of holiness. If any man sin, the first thing to do is to go to God and confess, "I have sinned." This is judging oneself, calling sin by its right name. "If we confess our sins, He is faithful and righteous to forgive us our sins, and to cleanse us from all unrighteousness." If you do this, you will then see that God forgives you and that your fellowship with Him is immediately restored.

15

4. The Way to Restoration

If a child of God should sin and continue in that sin without confession, he yet remains God's child and God is still his Father. Nevertheless, his fellowship with God will be lost. There is now a weakness in his conscience; he is unable to rise up before God. He may try to fellowship with God, but he will find it most painful and quite limited. It is just like a child who has done something wrong. Even though his mother may not know and may not scold him, he is still very uneasy at home. He finds it impossible to have sweet fellowship, for within him there is a sense of distance.

There is only one way to be restored. I must go to God and confess my sin. I believe that the Lord Jesus is my advocate and has taken care of all my sins. So here I am before God, humbly acknowledging my failure. I look to the Lord that hereafter I may not be so arrogant and careless. I have learned how prone I am to fall. I am no better than others. So I pray that God may be merciful to me, that I may continue on with the Lord step by step. Praise God, we do have an advocate with Him, One who does come alongside.

Prayer

O Lord, we ask You to instruct us. If it be possible, may these words be of profit to new believers. Lord, we are really concerned for their spiritual welfare. How we desire that new believers everywhere may go on well and glorify Your name. May they all be in the right path. May they learn some real lessons in the gospel so that they may be of use to You. Teach us how to help them and guide them.

16

We acknowledge that these words are fragmentary, as if of no great use, but we still look to You for mercy and grace. If You are merciful to us, we will be able to help them. We who are but nothing look to You for mercy, for we ask in the name of the Lord Jesus. Amen.

APOLOGY AND RESTITUTION

If any one sin, and commit a trespass against Jehovah, and deal falsely with his neighbor in a matter of deposit, or of bargain, or of robbery, or have oppressed his neighbor, or have found that which was lost, and deal falsely therein, and swear to a lie; in any of all these things that a man doeth, sinning therein; then it shall be, if he hath sinned, and is guilty, that he shall restore that which he took by robbery, or the thing which he hath gotten by oppression, or the deposit which was committed to him, or the lost thing which he found, or anything about which he hath sworn falsely; he shall even restore it in full, and shall add the fifth part more thereto: unto him to whom it appertaineth shall he give it, in the day of his being found guilty. And he shall bring his trespass-offering unto Jehovah, a ram without blemish out of the flock, according to thy estimation, for a trespass-offering, unto the priest: and the priest shall make atonement for him before Jehovah; and he shall be forgiven concerning whatsoever he doeth so as to be guilty thereby.

Lev. 6:2-7

If therefore thou art offering thy gift at the altar, and there rememberest that thy brother hath aught against thee, leave there thy gift before the altar, and go thy way, first be reconciled to thy brother, and then come and offer thy gift. Agree with thine adversary quickly, while thou art with him in the way; lest haply the adversary deliver thee to the judge, and the judge deliver thee to the officer, and thou be cast into prison. Verily I say unto thee, Thou shalt by no means come out thence, till thou have paid the last farthing.

Matt. 5:23–26

The Needed Habit of Apology and Restitution

After we believe in the Lord, we need to cultivate the habit of apologizing and making restitution. (We are not here referring to the things of the past. We have already dealt with that subject in Lesson 2.) If we offend or hurt anyone, we ought to learn to make amends for our fault either by an apology or by restitution. If we confess to God and apologize to men, our conscience will be kept sensitive and keen. Otherwise our conscience will become hard, and a hardened conscience is unable to receive God's light. Light does not shine easily upon a person with a hardened conscience.

The famous Welsh revivalist, Evan Roberts, always liked to ask people, "When was the last time you apologized?" If the last apology was a very long time ago, something must be wrong. It is inconceivable that one could live for years without offending someone. More likely, we have offended others without being conscious of our sins. If so, it proves that something is wrong with our conscience; it is in darkness, void of light and sensitivity.

"When was the last time you apologized?" By noticing

20

the length of the time lapse, we can know if there is anything between the person and his God. If the time lapse has been great, we know that his spirit lacks light. But if he has recently apologized to someone, then we know that his conscience is sensitive. New believers should see the importance of a sensitive conscience, for this alone enables us to live in God's light. With a sensitive conscience, we will continue to condemn our sins as sins. Many times we will have to confess our sins to God and also apologize to men.

Sins Requiring Apology

For what kind of sins do we need to apologize? Not all sins require an apology, but we should apologize for those which damage or hurt others. If I sin and what I do causes loss to my brother or to an unbeliever, I ought to express my regret to that person. I should not only confess to God but also apologize to the person involved.

We can ask God Himself to forgive us our sins, but how can we ask Him to forgive us on behalf of other people? Surely, we must confess to God and ask Him to forgive us, but also we should make it right with those whom we have hurt. It is very important that we never get the idea that to ask God alone for forgiveness is sufficient to cover up our offenses against others.

On the other hand, it is absolutely unnecessary to apologize for sins which are unrelated to men. May young believers be kept from overdoing, from going too far. Whatever sin is committed against God but is totally unassociated with man needs only to be confessed to God, but that which is a sin against man needs an apology to man.

For What to Apologize

How should we apologize for our sins? Let us have a good look at the trespass-offering of Leviticus 6. The trespass-offering has two sides: if anyone sins against man, he also sins against God. Every sin against man is also an affront to God. All sins come short of the glory of God: so the sinner must certainly offer a trespass-offering to God in confessing his sin.

The sin-offering and the trespass-offering are entirely different. The sin-offering deals with sin as a whole; it refers especially to the Day of Atonement, though not limited to only that day. It solves the problem of sin before God. The trespass-offering is more concerned with the many sins we commit such as sins against people. According to Leviticus 5, sins against man must also be confessed to God, and sacrifice needs to be offered for the remission of them.

But Leviticus 6 gives us further instruction about the trespass-offering. It shows us that as well as the offerings of sacrifices to God, there also ought to be dealings with the people whom we have offended. Though Leviticus 5 tells us how to deal with various sins before God by confessing and trusting in the cross for the remission of sins, yet the matter does not end there. If we have sinned against men, we have to clear up any such matter with the people whom we have offended. To see how this human side should be carried out, let us look a little more closely at Leviticus 6:2–7.

The trespass-offering requires that matters concerning other people have to be dealt with before there can be forgiveness. If things are not cleared up with men, forgiveness will not be granted. Therefore, a requirement of the trespass-offering is that whatever of a material nature is owed to people must be restored. We will now consider the specific items mentioned in Leviticus 6.

1. CARELESSNESS IN KEEPING THINGS

The first matter mentioned is things left in your hands for safekeeping by your neighbors. The things left are called a deposit in the Bible. God's children need to be careful about things deposited with them. If possible, it is better not to accept any deposit at all. If it is accepted, however, you must guard it carefully. If something should happen to it, you must be liable for the loss.

2. FALSE DEALINGS IN BARGAINING

One may deal falsely in bargaining as well as in things deposited. An example of falsehood in things deposited is if you keep what you like and give back something poorer. This is dealing falsely and is a trespass before God. In the matter of making a bargain, if you use any improper means (such as lying to gain a profit or to possess something which does not legally belong to you), then you have sinned before God. It is something that must be dealt with strictly.

3. ROBBERY

Though robbery is not likely to happen among the brethren, yet we should remind ourselves that no one ought to employ any method even resembling robbery. Taking advantage of one's position or authority or convenience to obtain that which is others' belongs in this category. Such things are sinful before God and man.

4. Oppression of One's Neighbor

We should in no way take advantage of any of our neighbors for self benefit, nor should we use position or power to oppress them or to show an arrogant attitude toward them. God's children ought not do these things, for they are sinful in the sight of God.

5. False Dealings in Lost Things

New believers should be especially careful in things that they find. Since they have not yet learned what righteousness is, they are prone to deal falsely with these lost articles. They may be tempted to take advantage of the situation by reducing the value or the amount or the condition of the found thing before returning it. They do this for their own benefit, but it is sinful before God.

6. Swearing to a Lie

To swear to any kind of a lie, pretending to have seen or not to have seen, to have known or not to have known, is definitely a sin which must be dealt with.

"In any of all these things that a man doeth, sinning therein"—this is the side of the trespass-offering which refers to our dealings with others. All the things mentioned in this passage are material things. I think the children of God need to learn a basic lesson—never try to twist things so as to make what belongs to others as one's own. It does not matter how you reason it out or how you change the thing; it simply is not right to take that which belongs to other people. What is theirs is theirs; it should not be made yours. To make it yours is incompatible with your Christian standing. Therefore, a new believer must learn from the very start of his Christian life to truthfully confess to God whatever sin he commits. If he deals falsely in any of the six ways mentioned above in order to profit, he has committed sin.

A Christian should not take things that others have lost. If he does find something, he must restore it to its owner. The law of the nation permits such things, allowing that after a certain period of time, the thing found becomes the finder's. But we Christians must restore what we have picked up; we should never consider it our own. If this is true of things we find, how much more must it be true of things gained through other means. It is wrong for us to turn another's possession into ours by any unrighteous means. As believers, we should not take advantage of others. To do so is a very bad habit.

We should learn to maintain a right conduct and a conscience without offense before God. How mighty is the Word of God here: "then it shall be, if he hath sinned, and is guilty, that he shall restore that which he took by robbery." The "restore" in the trespass-offering is connected with the "propitiate" in propitiation. A trespass-offering has two sides—to propitiate before God and to restore before man. Do not think that propitiation before God is enough; there must also be restoration to man. The trespass-offering mentioned in Leviticus 5 does not cover the human side because it is offered for sin which neither hurts others nor causes their material loss. Hence, there is no need to restore anything. But in Leviticus 6 there is physical or material damage involved; therefore we believers must make restoration. "He shall even restore it in full," says the Word of God.

25

How to Restore

We have previously mentioned that many things which we did before we believed in the Lord need to be thoroughly taken care of. Now we must also say that any unrighteousness which we may commit after we believe must also be dealt with. It is possible not to sin; but if we sin, we must confess to God. Through the Lord our Mediator, as typified by the ashes of the red heifer, our fellowship with God can be restored. If we have anything belonging to another, we must restore it; we cannot turn someone else's possession into our own.

The question is: how shall we restore it? "He shall even restore it in full, and shall add the fifth part more thereto: unto him to whom it appertaineth shall he give it, in the day of his being found guilty" (v. 5). There are five points we should consider.

1. THE RULE OF RESTORATION

First, it must be restored. No one can say, "Everything is fine," just because he has confessed his sin if he still keeps in his home what belongs to someone else. As long as another's possession is in his home, he manifestly is in the wrong.

2. THE PRINCIPLE OF RESTORATION

God desires us to restore in full and to add one-fifth more. Why should this fifth part be added? The principle is that you restore fully. God does not want His children to do just barely enough in anything. He wants us to leave a wide margin. In apologizing or making restitution, we should not calculate too closely but, rather, should be generous and full.

26

CONFESS LIBERALLY

I feel the confession of some people is far short of the extra fifth part. When such a person confesses, he will say he is wrong on *this* point and therefore he apologizes; on *that* point, though, he has not sinned but rather has been sinned against. I tell you, this is not confession but balancing accounts! I am wrong in saying this, but you are wrong in saying that—this is balancing accounts. So, in making apology, do not be stingy. Apologize more rather than less. No one told you to sin; in order to restore, why not restore more? This is the right spirit of confession. Do not restore only as much as you have taken. God's children should do more than just barely enough.

RETAIN POSITION AS CHILD OF GOD

Whatever a child of God does, he needs to maintain his status as a child of God. To apologize as if one were balancing accounts is the apology of worldlings; it is not the way for God's children. A child of God needs to acknowledge his sin with candor and add a fifth part in the restitution. One should not be calculating in confession. To complete how much I owe you and how much you owe me is really not Christian. "I originally was not angry. It was your word which made me angry. I will confess my anger, but you must also confess your harsh words"—again this is balancing accounts. In apology, let us be generous rather than stingy.

ADD THE FIFTH PART

I believe there is a definite benefit in adding a fifth part. It helps to keep you from committing the same act the second time since it is a losing proposition. New believers especially need to learn that they may appear to win temporarily but actually they lose out afterward. What you took was five-fifths, but what you must restore is six-fifths. When you took it, you seemed to gain, but when you restore it, the Lord says, "Restore it in full and . . . add the fifth part more thereto."

3. THE TIME FOR RESTORATION

Apology and restitution should be made at the first opportunity. The Word here says, "Unto him to whom it appertaineth shall he give it, in the day of his being found guilty." If it is within your ability and the thing is still there, you should restore it on the day of your being found guilty. It is very easy to postpone these things. Because of postponing it, many children of God find their sensitivity dulled. When you receive light and find yourself guilty, that is the time you should act. It is best if things are restored on the same day. May new believers be kept in this straight path. Never try to take advantage of other people, for to do so makes you unrighteous. A basic principle of our Christian life here on earth is never to profit at another's expense. It is wrong to take advantage of others. May new believers learn to be righteous from the start.

I know of some places where the brothers and sisters have the habit of making public restitution. I do not approve of the kind of public confession done in some revival meetings. I do not believe that what offends an individual should be confessed in public. But I do believe that every unrighteous act must be dealt with; otherwise God's children will be wanting in the sense of righteousness. This will cause them to have a guilty conscience before God and thus reduce the light needed for their path. We must, therefore, pay attention to this matter.

4. Seeking God's Forgiveness

Please remember that apology or restitution alone is still insufficient. The case is not yet closed, for there is something more to be done. "And he shall bring his trespass-offering unto Jehovah, a ram without blemish out of the flock, according to thy estimation, for a trespass-offering, unto the priest" (v. 6). The trespass-offering in Leviticus 5 covers only the dealings before God, because no trouble with man has been incurred. But in chapter 6, the person has sinned against man, so he needs to deal with the sin first before man and then go to God for forgiveness. Unless it is first settled with man, there is no way of going to God and asking for forgiveness. One must first restore what he has taken; then he can receive forgiveness from God. After the ram without blemish has been offered to the Lord as a trespass-offering, then "the priest shall make atonement for him before Jehovah; and he shall be forgiven concerning whatsoever he doeth so as to be guilty thereby" (v. 7).

5. A Lifetime Practice

This is a matter of prime importance. We need to do our best to restore whatever we owe people materially and then come to seek forgiveness from the Lord through His blood. Do not despise this as being too elementary. It may surprise you to find that such offenses are quite prevalent everywhere, and that they are steadily increasing in number. If we are a little careless, we can easily take advantage of other people. Hence, it should be a lifetime practice for God's children to restore whatever thing is not theirs.

The Practice of Matthew 5

Now let us turn to the second passage of the Scriptures. It is found in Matthew 5. There is a difference between Matthew 5 and Leviticus 6. Leviticus 6 deals only with material indebtedness, while Matthew 5 is wider in its application.

1. DEAL WITH ALL INDEBTEDNESS

The last farthing in Matthew 5 does not refer to an actual amount of money; rather, it suggests that if any indebtedness is not cleared the person is still not free.

FIRST BE RECONCILED TO YOUR BROTHER

Let us look more closely at this passage. "If therefore thou art offering thy gift at the altar, and there rememberest that thy brother hath aught against thee"—here it refers especially to matters among God's children, matters between brother and brother. It is when you are offering your gift at the altar, not when you are praying. At that very time you remember that your brother has something against you. This, indeed, is God's guidance. Frequently, in matters of this nature, the Holy Spirit recalls a certain incident or puts an appropriate thought into your mind. When it comes, do not push the thought aside as if it were merely something fleeting. Rather, deal faithfully with it.

When you remember how your brother feels it must be because you have offended him. Such indebtedness may or may not be material in character; nonetheless it is an indebtedness. You may have offended him by an unrighteous act pertaining either to material or nonmaterial things; if so, then he has something against you. Should a brother or a person whom you have offended moan and grieve before God because of you, then you are seriously hampered in God's sight.

As a new believer, you should see that if you do not apologize and ask forgiveness from the person against whom you sinned, you will be adversely affected if he mentions your name with sighing before God. All the gifts which you offer to God will not be accepted; all your prayers will not be heard. Therefore, you must be very careful lest your brother sigh before God because of you. His sigh renders you useless. Your way before God is blocked. He whom you have troubled does not need to accuse you in the presence of God; he needs only to say to God, "Alas, this person," and all your offerings are rejected, all your sacrifices and prayers are left unheard. His "Alas, this person" is quite enough to upset things for you. So let us never give opportunity or ground to any brother or sister to sigh before God for our sake. If so, our spiritual way will be obstructed and all our offerings will become useless.

If, when about to offer your gift at the altar, you remember that a brother has something against you, it is better that you do not proceed. Leave your gift, for it is right to leave it with God with a view to offering it later. "First be reconciled to thy brother, and then come and offer thy gift." Though the gift is for God, there must first be reconciliation with man. Whoever fails to be reconciled to man cannot come to God and offer. "Be reconciled with thy brother"—what does it mean? It means to appease his wrath, whether by apology or by making restitution. You must apologize or repay until he is reasonably satisfied.

31

The problem here is no longer the added fifth part, sixth part, or third part; it is the matter of reconciliation. Reconciliation implies satisfaction of the offended.

Because you have sinned against him, you are thus indebted to him. You have caused him to feel that you are unrighteous, so he sighs before God on account of you. Let me tell you, this cuts off all your communication with God. Even though you may not be aware of your darkness, you nevertheless find it impossible to offer your gift on the altar. Not only are you unable to ask God for anything, but also you are unable to even give something to God. Not only can you not ask God to come down, but also you are unable to offer Him anything. Everything is on the altar, but God will accept none of it. For this reason, you must satisfy your brother before you come to the altar. Whatever may be your brother's demand, try your very best, within reason, to satisfy him. You should learn to satisfy your brother's righteous request as well as God's righteous demand. You must satisfy your brother to the point that you can offer your gift to God. This is, indeed, quite a serious matter.

AGREE WITH YOUR ADVERSARY QUICKLY

Do not easily offend people, especially do not offend a brother. But if you do, you will fall under a judgment from which it is hard to be extricated. The Lord puts it emphatically, "Agree with thine adversary quickly while thou art with him in the way." How? "While thou art with him in the way." Today we all are yet in the way. Neither he nor you has died. Both of you are living and therefore yet in the way. So make up with him quickly.

There will come a day when either you or he will not be in the way. Who knows which one of you will go first? It will be too late then. So while you both are yet in the way, while there is still opportunity to talk and to apologize, you should agree with him quickly. We know the door of salvation is not open forever. Likewise, the door of apology is not always open. Sometimes a brother may repent, yet have no opportunity to apologize because the other party is no longer in the way. Therefore, seize the opportunity while both are yet in the way. Be reconciled to him. Confession and spiritual life are two closely linked things. The time to be reconciled is now. If one of the two parties is not in the way, reconciliation can no longer be carried out.

How serious this matter is. We cannot afford to be careless about it. Let us learn before God to be reconciled with our brother today. We should not postpone it. We should take note if any brother complains against us. If we are wrong, we should try our best to apologize lest we miss the chance of reconciliation.

The Lord follows with a human illustration: "Lest haply the adversary deliver thee to the judge, and the judge deliver thee to the officer, and thou shalt be cast into prison. Verily I say unto thee, thou shalt by no means come out thence, till thou have paid the last farthing." I cannot go into details. It is possible that this is somewhat related to the kingdom. We do not, however, stress the interpretation of the last farthing, but we do want to notice its practical implication. The payment of the last farthing indicates that this matter, whatever it is, must be fully solved before God. The case will not be removed until it is fully paid. The purpose of the Lord here is not to teach us how we will be judged in the future, or how we will be imprisoned, or how we shall get out of prison. None of these is the Lord's emphasis here. He insists only that we must be reconciled today. Today the last farthing must be paid; do not wait until the future. Do it while in the way. Do not postpone it. The Lord clearly shows us that it does not pay to leave it to the future.

2. LEARN DILIGENTLY

The children of God must diligently learn to make restitution where restitution is due and to apologize where apology is needed. All who learn to serve God should pay special attention to this matter. It is safe to apologize and to make reparation constantly. To not be in a very clear place in this matter is unwise. We should never allow brothers and sisters to have any complaint against us. Unless our conscience is clear and we have not done any wrong, we should acknowledge each of our faults. We should be blameless in our conduct. It cannot be that we are always right and others are always wrong. For us to always say we are right when others complain against us just will not do.

How to Apologize and Make Restitution

Now, let us see how we should apologize and how we should make restitution.

1. THE SCOPE

In this matter of making apology or restitution, the sin itself determines the scope of the apology or of the restitution. We do not want people to go to extremes. We desire that brothers and sisters act in accordance with God's Word and not be excessive. It is in excessiveness that Satan has ground to launch his attack. The scope of the apology should be as wide as the scope of the sin. If the sin is against all, then confess to all. If the sin is against one person, confess only to that person. To confess to one person when the sin is against all is not sufficient; to confess to all when the sin is against only one person is overdoing it. The scope of the sin determines the scope of the confession. Of course, giving testimony is another matter. I have sinned in a personal way frequently, but sometimes I want to testify about it to brothers and sisters. This is something else again, to be treated separately. But as for apology and restitution, these two are definite in their scope. This point must be carefully observed.

2. UNRIGHTEOUS TO INCRIMINATE OTHERS

If two people sin together, say for example, stealing or using falsehood to obtain something, then the one who apologizes or makes restitution should not incriminate the other. Whatever knowledge we have is a trust. He who violates a trust in unrighteous. If anyone informs me of a certain matter, it is like entrusting me with a sum of money. I cannot sell my trust because it would be unrighteous. Remember, it is unrighteous for you to reveal any trust that people confide to you. So, in making apology or restitution, do not incriminate the other person lest you be unrighteous.

3. SINS NOT TO BE CONFESSED

There are certain sins which should not be confessed. You should not confess for the sake of appeasing your own conscience if the one who hears your confession will lose his peace as a result. To make yourself peaceful but to take away another's peace should not be done. For example: Suppose a girl did something terribly wrong, sinning against her mother, but her mother was unaware of it. Her mother, though a church member, is uncertain of her salvation, and, besides, has a fierce temper. The daughter, having been enlightened by God, is convicted of her sin. She feels terribly bad about it and is constantly troubled by it. So she tells her mother about the sinful thing she did against her. After the confession, the daughter has peace in her heart. But the mother, since that day, becomes so disturbed that she loses her temper and rants day and night. The mother loses her peace while the daughter regains hers. The principle is: never gain your peace at the price of another's peace.

4. CONSULT THE RESPONSIBLE BROTHERS

In making apology, new believers should learn to frequently consult the responsible brothers of the church. Thus, the new believers, under the protection of the church can carry out their task properly and without excess. Confer with the responsible brothers so that they may instruct you as to what things should be confessed and what things need not be.

5. THE RESPONSIBILITY OF THE CHURCH

The church, especially the workers and the responsible brothers, should instruct new believers as to how to deal with matters which require apology or restitution. Many sins should be throughly confessed, but some sins should only be indirectly referred to lest they hurt others.

6. AN EXTREME CASE

I know of a case concerning a sister and her sister-in-law. The latter did many harmful things behind the back of the sister, but the sister did not know the source of these bad things. Later on, the sister-in-law confessed to the sister, and the case became more serious. Many unpleasant things followed. Had the sister-in-law merely said that she was sorry for saying many words and doing many things against the sister, there might not have been any serious consequences. But unfortunately she confessed the details. True, she was cleared of a guilty conscience thereafter, but the opposite party slid into committing many sins.

None of us should fall into such an error. The responsible brothers should teach the brethren how to confess properly. Some matters may be explained in detail but others should only be mentioned. Some people can be told everything, but to others no details should be given. There is a great difference in this.

7. LETTERS OF RESTITUTION

Concerning restitution, it is possible that you may not have the ability to repay. To make restitution is one thing, to be able to repay is another thing. If you do not have the ability to reimburse, you still must write a letter of restitution. You can honestly write: "I will repay but am unable to do it just now. Please forgive me. As soon as I am able, I will immediately pay back." This, too, ought to be done.

8. IF NO WAY

If a person has passed away, he obviously cannot accept your restitution. According to the Old Testament, in such a case you should deliver your restitution to the Levites. By the same principle, if today there is no recipient for your repayment, then give it to the church. But if there is a legal recipient, the church cannot accept it for the wronged party. If that person has passed away, then give it to his relative; if there is no relative, give it to the church.

Though it may be easier for you, you cannot give it to the church as long as there is a proper recipient.

As to apology, if the person has already died, you should confess the thing to the church according to the principle described above. You should express your willingness to apologize and you should ask for the mercy of God.

9. DIFFICULTIES SOLVED

The church needs to make special arrangements for these matters. The church should help brothers and sisters to make apologies and restitutions properly. Each one of us must have a right spiritual condition. We must neither incriminate other people, nor should we escape our responsibility. We must apologize and make restitution. When we need help, we should ask the responsible brothers of the church for it, so that we may discharge these duties. With the church involved, we will be delivered from excess.

10. CONSCIENCE CLEANSED

Finally, it is important that one not fall under excessive accusation because of making apologies. This is something quite possible. Each person needs to see how the blood of the Lord cleanses his conscience. Through His death, one can have a conscience void of offense before God. The Lord's death enables him to draw nigh to God. Such is the reality. On the other side, he must also see that in order to be a clean person in the sight of the world, he has to deal with his many sins. Whether he sins against people in material things or in other matters, he should be ready to deal with it. Never, however, allow Satan to attack with excessive accusation.

"Confess therefore your sins one to another" (Jas.

38

5:16a). The result? "That ye may be healed." Frequently God's children are sick because of the presence of disturbing matters among them. When they confess one to another, their sickness is healed. May new believers always keep themselves clean by confessing their sins continuously to God and by clearing up all matters of offense with men. Thus their consciences will be strong and good.

RESTORE YOUR BROTHER

One problem that must be solved is, what should we do if someone sins against us? The question under consideration now is not what should we do if we sin against others, but what should we do if people sin against us. Let us read Matthew 18:15–35, for this passage gives special instruction on the subject.

And if thy brother sin against thee, go, show him his fault between thee and him alone: if he hear thee, thou has gained thy brother. But if he hear thee not, take with thee one or two more, that at the mouth of two witnesses or three every word may be established. And if he refuse to hear them, tell it unto the church: and if he refuse to hear the church also, let him be unto thee as the Gentile and the publican. Verily I say unto you, What things soever ye shall bind on earth shall be bound in heaven; and what things soever ye shall loose on earth shall be loosed in heaven. Again I say unto you, that if two of you shall agree on earth as touching anything that they shall ask, it shall be done for them of my Father who is in heaven. For where two or three are gathered together in my name, there am I in the midst of them.

Then came Peter and said to him, Lord, how oft shall my brother sin against me, and I forgive him? until seven times? Jesus saith unto him, I say not unto thee, Until seven times; but, Until seventy times seven. Therefore is the kingdom of heaven likened unto a certain king, who would make a reckoning with his servants. And when he had begun to reckon, one was brought unto him, that owed him ten thousand talents. But forasmuch as he had not wherewith to pay, his lord commanded him to be sold, and his wife, and children, and all that he had, and payment to be made. The servant therefore fell down, and worshipped him, saying, Lord, have patience with me, and I will pay thee all. And the lord of that servant, being moved with compassion, released him, and forgave him the debt. But that servant went out, and found one of his fellow-servants, who owed him a hundred shillings: and he laid hold on him, and took him by the throat, saying, Pay what thou owest. So his fellow-servant fell down and besought him, saying, Have patience with me, and I will pay thee. And he would not: but went and cast him into prison, till he should pay that which was due. So when his fellow-servants saw what was done, they were exceeding sorry, and came and told unto their lord all that was done. Then his lord called him unto him, and saith to him, Thou wicked servant, I forgave thee all that debt, because thou besought me: shouldest not thou also have had mercy on thy fellow-servant, even as I had mercy on thee? And his lord was wroth, and delivered him to the tormentors, till he should pay all that was due. So shall also my heavenly Father do unto you, if ye forgive not every one his brother from your hearts.

Matt. 18:15–35

In analyzing this passage, we find it can be divided into two parts: forgiveness (vv. 21–35), and persuasion (vv.

15–20). The Lord tells us that if our brother should sin against us, our first responsibility is to forgive him before God, and our second responsibility is to persuade him before God. We often mention the first matter of forgiveness, but we should equally emphasize the second matter of persuasion.

The First Responsibility—Forgiveness

"Then came Peter and said to Him, Lord, how oft shall my brother sin against me, and I forgive him? until seven times?" (v. 21). We find this not only in Matthew but also in Luke. And Luke records it a little differently.

1. FORGIVE BOUNDLESSLY

"Take heed to yourselves: if thy brother sin, rebuke him; and if he repent, forgive him. And if he sin against thee seven times in the day, and seven times turn again to thee, saying, I repent; thou shalt forgive him" (Luke 17:3–4). This is similar to Matthew's record but not entirely the same. The words in Matthew seem to be weightier. Forgiveness there is not to be given seven times, but seventy times seven. "Seventy times seven" means that the forgiveness the children of God extend toward their brethren is to be unlimited. There is no counting the number of times, for it is not seven times but seventy times seven.

The point which Luke stresses is that if the brother who sins against us repents and asks for forgiveness, we must forgive even if it is seven times in one day. The question is not whether his repentance is true or false. We are to disregard that. If he says he repents, we forgive and leave the matter of repentance with him.

43

To forgive the same thing seven times during a longer period of time may not seem too much, but to forgive it seven times in one day is something else. The same thing happens seven times in the same day by the same person and each time he comes, saying, "I am sorry." Do you believe his apology is sincere? Perhaps you feel he is just paying lip service. No wonder it says in the following verse, "The apostles said unto the Lord, Increase our faith" (v. 5). Having forgiven the offending one so many times, they lost their faith. They really felt it was a problem. It seemed inconceivable that the same person could genuinely come seven times in the day to ask for forgiveness. They could hardly believe it was sincere. They lost their faith. So they asked the Lord to increase their faith. God's answer, though, is that His children must forgive even under such trying circumstances. We must not refrain from forgiving; we must not continue to remember the sin of him who has offended us.

2. Forgive Generously

The Lord then uses a parable.

Therefore is the kingdom of heaven likened unto a certain king, who would make a reckoning with his servants. And when he had begun to reckon, one was brought unto him, that owed him ten thousand talents. But forasmuch as he had not wherewith to pay, his lord commanded him to be sold, and his wife, and children, and all that he had, and payment to be made. The servant therefore fell down, and worshipped him, saying, Lord, have patience with me, and I will pay thee all. And the lord of that servant, being moved with compassion, released him, and forgave him the debt.

Matt. 18:23–27

There are a few special points that require our attention. What we owe forever exceeds what we can repay. We owe God ten thousand talents, far beyond our ability to pay back for we have nothing with which to repay. All of us need to have a right estimate of our own indebtedness to God so that we may generously forgive our brother's debt. If we forget how great the grace we have received from God, we then become the most ungracious of men. In order to see how little people owe us, we need to see how much we owe God.

The servant in the parable owed his lord ten thousand talents. It was a tremendous sum of money, and he had no way of repaying "forasmuch as he had not wherewith to pay." Do remember that man's indebtedness to God is always beyond his ability to repay. The difference between what people owe us and what we owe God is exceedingly great. Even though the master ordered "him to be sold, and his wife, and children, and all that he had," even so the payment could never be made. "The servant therefore fell down and worshipped him, saying, Lord, have patience with me, and I will pay thee all."

ACCORDING TO GOD'S MEASURE

Men never really know what grace is. We do not understand clearly what the gospel is. Our tendency is to say to God that what we cannot do today, we will do later on. How absurd for the servant to plead for time when the proceeds from selling both himself and all that he had could not possibly repay the debt. He pleaded, "Lord, have patience with me, and I will pay thee all." It was as if he were saying, "Give me time. My intention is good. I am not thinking of evading my debt. I only ask for more time so that I can pay back." Salvation, though, does not come according to man's thought but according to God's measure.

We love to see people pray, and we love especially to see how God answers prayer. His answer, though, is not necessarily according to the prayer. God hears prayer, but He may not hear what we ask for! The robber on the cross prayed, "Jesus, remember me when thou comest in thy kingdom." The Lord heard him pray, but He did not answer him as he had prayed. The Lord replied, "Today shalt thou be with me in Paradise" (Lk. 23:42–43). God saves us according to His idea, not according to the sinner's idea. Salvation does not follow man's limited thought as to how God should save him. Rather, it is formulated by God's own thought as to what He would like to do. The Lord wanted the repentant robber to be with Him in paradise that day; He did not want to wait till the kingdom comes before remembering him.

The publican prayed in the temple, smiting his breast and saying, "God, be thou merciful to me a sinner" (see Lk. 18:9–14). At most he could only plead for mercy. God heard him, but not according to his prayer, for the Lord Jesus said, "This man went down to his house justified." Do you see how this far exceeds what a sinner could think of? A sinner asks for mercy; he would never think of justification. But God said that the man was justified. It meant that he had never sinned; not only was he not sinful, but also he actually was righteous. Not only were his sins forgiven, but also he went home justified. The salvation which the Lord accomplishes is not according to man's thought, but according to His own thought.

The return of the prodigal son tells the same story. Upon his return home, he asked to be made as one of the hired servants. Even while he was still in the distant land, before he met his father, he prepared to come home as a servant. But when he got home, he never was made one of the servants. The father put the best robe on him, a ring on his hand and shoes on his feet, and also killed the fatted calf to celebrate his return. I like the word "the," for it specifies the fattest of all the fatted calves. The father ordered the fatted calf, the calf which everyone knew, to be brought and killed and eaten. He called in all the neighbors and friends to join in the eating and the merry-making, "for this my son was dead, and is alive again; he was lost, and is found" (see Lk. 15:11–32). Let me tell you, God has not done according to the sinner's thought but according to His own thought.

Several people carried a man sick of the palsy to the Lord Jesus. They expected the Lord to heal the palsied. The Lord heard them but not according to their specific request. They hoped to see the palsied walk, but the Lord Jesus said, "Son, thy sins are forgiven" (see Mk. 2:1–12). What, then, is the gospel? The gospel is that God will work until He Himself is satisfied. Let us, then, bring people to God and pray for them. It really does not matter much whether we pray well or not, for God will work till He satisfies Himself. He will not just satisfy the sinner; He must satisfy Himself. In the prodigal's thought, bread to eat is quite enough. But what is sufficient for the prodigal is not sufficient for the father. Salvation must be accomplished to the satisfaction of the Father, not just to that of the prodigal son. We need to view salvation from God's viewpoint.

The servant pleaded with his master, "Be patient with me, for I will pay back. I will try my best. I will pay back in the future. Maybe I can repay all." Whoever approaches God and asks for grace, to him grace will be given even though he knows very little of what grace is. This is a principle we must see—the Lord delights to give grace. If you express even a slight desire for grace, grace will be given to you. The Lord only fears our not asking. A person who hopes for mercy shall receive mercy. God will give grace till His own heart is satisfied. You may ask for a dollar, for that much is quite enough for you; but He will not give you a dollar—He will give you a thousand dollars. He must work till He Himself is satisfied. He cannot deny Himself. If He gives, He gives according to His own nature.

The servant said he would repay in the future. "And the lord of that servant, being moved with compassion, released him, and forgave him the debt." Do you see that this is the gospel? God does not do things according to your wish. After you say, "Lord, have patience with me, allow me to pay back little by little till all is paid," the Lord does not answer with, "All right. Pay what you have now and clear up the rest in the days to come." Let me tell you, our prayer for grace is never big enough. When I study the Bible, I come away with the feeling that all our prayers and supplications fall far short of what the Lord has given us. Our Lord hears our prayers according to what He has, and He works for us accordingly. What we have prayed for is included in His answer, *but,* He also does far more than that. The master released the servant and forgave him all the debt. This was far beyond the servant's request. God always does exceedingly abundantly above all that we ask or think. This is the grace of God.

HAVING RECEIVED GRACE, LEARN
TO BE GRACIOUS

But God has a purpose in being gracious to us. All who themselves need grace ought to learn the outworking of grace. All who have received grace should learn to be gracious to others. God expects the recipients of His grace to be gracious. He does not look for righteousness alone but also for graciousness. "But that servant went out, and found one of his fellow-servants, who owed him a hundred shillings: and he laid hold on him, and took him by the throat, saying, Pay what thou owest. So his fellow-servant fell down and besought him, saying, Have patience with me, and I will pay thee" (Matt. 18:28–29). The Lord shows us here that there is no comparison between what we owe Him and what others owe us. What we owe is ten thousand talents ($10,000,000), but what others owe us is only a hundred shillings ($20.00). When we plead with the Lord, "O Lord, have patience with us, for we will pay back some day," the Lord forgives us the debt. He does not listen to the second part of our prayer, though, because He has fully forgiven.

After this you meet your companion, your brother, who, however much he may have offended you, at the most can only owe you one hundred shillings. He owes you that little, and he also pleads with you to be patient with him for he will some day pay you back. His prayer and his expectation are the same as yours had been—some time in which to pay back. Yet the servant in the parable refused to be gracious. "And he would not: but went and cast him into prison, till he should pay that which was due" (Matt. 18:30).

The Lord uses this parable to illustrate how unreasonable an unforgiving person is in the sight of God. If you do not forgive your brother, you are that man, even as Nathan had to tell David, "Thou art the man" (2 Sam. 12:7). When we read this parable in Matthew 18, we feel how unreasonable that servant was. We feel, "How could this man refuse the pleading of his companion and put him in jail for the payment of one hundred shillings when he himself has been forgiven by his lord of his debt of ten thousand talents?" Yes, the servant was righteous to demand payment, but a believer's life with other people is not based on righteousness but on graciousness. It certainly does not mean that your brother does not owe you anything, for the Lord also knows that he does. Yet the Lord wants us to see clearly that if a believer does not forgive another believer, he is not acting according to grace. In God's eye he lacks grace.

The principle which should govern the fellowship of believers is grace. It is not that your companion owes you nothing; but if you put him in jail, the Lord will immediately put you in jail. His debt is real, but so is yours. The basis for believers' fellowship is not righteousness but grace. The Bible teaches that we ought to be righteous as to what we owe others; as to what others owe us, though, we must not ask for righteousness but should learn to be gracious. When a believer offends you and owes you something, there is only one rule for you: you must give grace.

HAVING RECEIVED MERCY, BE MERCIFUL

So when his fellow-servants saw what was done, they were exceeding sorry, and came and told unto their lord all that was done. Then his lord called him unto him, and saith to him, Thou wicked servant, I forgave thee all that debt, because thou besoughtest me: shouldest not thou also have had mercy on thy fellow-servant, even as I had mercy on thee?

Matt. 18:31–33

The Lord expects you to treat others as He has treated you. Since He does not demand of you according to righteousness, He expects you not to demand righteousness of others. The Lord forgives your debt according to mercy. With what measure He has meted out to you, He wants you to mete out to others. He gives you in good measure, pressed down, shaken together and running over; He wishes you to do likewise. As He treats you, so should you treat your brother.

It is exceedingly ugly in the sight of God for the forgiven person to be unforgiving. Nothing can be uglier than for the one who was forgiven to be unforgiving, the one who received mercy to be merciless, and the one who was given grace to be graceless. We must learn before God to treat others as He has treated us. Let us be so humbled by what we have received that we treat others according to the same principle.

We can find many things in the Bible which God dislikes. One of these that He most dislikes is for His children to be unwilling to forgive. It is shameful for those who have received grace and forgiveness to refuse to be gracious and forgiving. For the debtor to exact a debt is something God condemns. For the offended one to remember the offense is something God hates.

May we hear what the lord asked the servant: "Shouldest not thou also have had mercy on thy fellow-servant, even as I had mercy on thee?" God desires us to be like Him in this respect.

"And his lord was wroth, and delivered him to the tormentors, till he should pay all that was due" (Matt. 18:34). Here the servant fell into the governmental discipline of his master who delivered him to the tormentors till he should pay all.

"So shall also your heavenly Father do unto you, if ye forgive not everyone his brother from your hearts" (Matt.

18:35). May none of us fall into the governmental hand of God. We must forgive our brother from our heart as God has forgiven us. We must not remember other's sins, nor should we seek for payment. Though it is righteous to do so, yet it is sinful. The children of God ought to be like God in extending generosity.

The Second Responsibility—Persuasion

I believe many of God's children have learned the lesson of forgiveness. Many, though, have forgotten what we should do after someone has sinned against us. According to Matthew 18:15–20, we must persuade or exhort our brother. We must not only forgive but we must persuade as well.

1. TELL HIM

"And if thy brother sin against thee" (v. 15). It is quite common for God's children to sin against one another. Although such things may not happen too often, neither are they too scarce. The Lord shows us what we should do if anyone sins against us. "Go, show him his fault between thee and him alone." Should anyone sin against you, the first thing to do is to tell him, not to tell others. This is a word we should rightly understand. Show his fault to him when you and he are alone.

Therefore, when your brother sins against you, do not tell it to other brothers and sisters. Do not at this point go to the responsible brothers of the church either. The Lord has not even commanded you to tell God about it in prayer. New believers should be clear about this: when a brother sins against you, the first thing you should do is to go and tell him. I believe if the children of God kept this commandment of the Lord, many, perhaps half, of the problems in the church would be solved.

Today's difficulty is that soon after a brother has sinned against another brother, the matter becomes known to everyone, except to the one who has sinned. The offended brother has broadcast it everywhere. This indicates how weak he is, for it is only the weak who will tell tales. He is morally weak since he has not the strength to tell the offender. He can only backbite; he has not the courage to speak face to face. To broadcast and to spread rumors is a bad, unclean, sinful habit. We need to take care of our brother's fault, not tell others. The first person to be told ought to be the offender himself—no one else. If God's children learn this lesson well, the church will be delivered from many difficulties.

The Lord says, "Show him his fault." But how? The Lord does not suggest you write a letter but that you go to him. Talk to him when you and he are alone. This is the Lord's command. In dealing with personal sin, the two of you are sufficient; a third party is absolutely unnecessary.

Let us learn this lesson before God. We must control ourselves and never speak behind the back of the brother who has offended us. Nor should we speak in public against him. It is only when you and he are alone that you show him his fault. This requires the grace of God. When you speak, you are to show him his fault, not to talk about other things. To point out his fault is not an easy thing to do, but you have to do it. This is one of the lessons which the children of God must learn. Go to him and say, "Brother, you hurt me by doing such a thing. It was wrong for you to do it. You have sinned."

If you feel the matter is so small that it does not require

53

you to go and tell him, then it also does not warrant your telling anybody else. I have heard many complain that to follow this rule is very troublesome. Too many things happen daily for us to go and tell the offenders. Well, if you feel a matter is not important, only a small matter which need not be told to the offender, then I say it also need not be told to anybody else. How can you say it need not be told to the person himself yet you tell it to others? If it is necessary, tell the brother himself; otherwise, do not tell it at all. To do so is a sin.

PURPOSE: TO GAIN YOUR BROTHER

God's children should learn to overlook offenses. But if an offense must be dealt with, deal with the offender directly. In such dealing, we need to remember this fundamental principle: "If he hear thee, thou hast gained thy brother" (v 15). This is the purpose of telling. The motive is not to lessen your difficulty nor to demand reparation from the offender. The purpose is to gain your brother.

Thus the problem is not how greatly I have suffered or even how far I can restore my brother. I go to persuade him because if he does not clear up this matter, he will have trouble with his prayer and fellowship with God.

If it is merely a matter of your hurt feelings, then it is too small a thing to require dealing. You need to see clearly before God as to which matters require your dealing with your brother and which do not. If it is only your hurt feelings, you may let it pass without telling your brother or anybody else. Whether or not it is more than that, no one knows better than you. Even the elders of the church do not know better. The responsibility is upon you. Some matters have great effect. There are many things which you can forget but there are certain matters which you should not. If your brother has sinned with the possibility that he will suffer loss, you must go to him and point out his fault when you and he are alone. That which cannot be casually dismissed has to be dealt with. How can he get by if there is something unforgiven between him and God?

God's children should learn to rid the church of problems, not to add problems to the church. We must seek to keep the oneness of the church. If you see a brother in a fault which creates a problem before the Lord, you know this is not a small matter. You feel this will hinder him from going on with the Lord. In such a case you should find an opportunity to speak to him when you two are alone. Tell him, "Brother, it was wrong for you to sin against me in this way. As a consequence, your way before God will be blocked. Your loss is great." If he hears you, the Lord says, "Thou hast gained thy brother," for you have restored a soul.

The purpose of persuasion is to restore. It is not for reparation, nor for easing your feeling, but to restore your brother. Let me tell you, this passage in Scripture is one least obeyed by the children of God. What do we do instead? Some of us talk and broadcast the matter; some keep the thing in their hearts and refuse to forgive; some simply forgive and do nothing more. But none of these is what the Lord would have us do.

The Lord does not say if your brother sins against you, you may just disregard it. The Lord says that in sinning, your brother has created a problem, and you, the offended, have a responsibility toward him. He has sinned against you, but you must think of his future. You must fulfill your Christian duty by going and speaking to him.

Since you are the only one who knows your brother is wrong, you must try to restore him so as to gain your brother. Your attitude must be good; your motive must be right. You are to restore your brother; you hope to gain him. If your motive is to gain him, you will know how to point out his fault. But if you do not desire to restore him, you will probably quarrel. Formerly it was he who quarreled with you, but now you quarrel with each other. So the purpose of talking to him is not merely to point out his fault but, rather, to gain him. The Lord has not said if your brother sins against you, go and scold him. He says go and talk to him in order to gain him.

If the motive is right, you will have no trouble to know how you should proceed. In order to gain your brother, how necessary it is that your words, attitude, expression, voice, tone, manner, and spirit all be right. Remember, an enemy may know my fault, but only a brother can gain me. What my enemy says may be true; I cannot deny that his words are true. Yet however true his words may be, he has no way to gain me.

Perhaps someone comes to scold and reprimand you. His reproach is justifiable; even his sharpest words are true. But his attitude and facial expression do not gain you. It is easy to know a person's fault, but to gain him by pointing out his fault is quite another matter. Anyone may get angry. You do not need grace to lose your temper. How deceived we are to think that we are demonstrating the wrath of righteousness.

It is not a difficult task to make people know their sins, for even enemies can do it. But it needs a brother to make us know our sins and at the same time to restore us. Only a brother can tenderly show us our fault as well as our condition before the Lord. This is the responsibility of believers.

I have a heavy burden within me as I realize how many times the children of God fail to follow the Lord's Word with regard to offenses. This is an exceedingly delicate thing which we need to learn today. I think it is quite easy to praise a brother; anyone who wants to can do it without difficulty. It is also easy to lose one's temper with a brother; with a little less control over our emotions we can pour it out on our brother. But letting a brother know his fault while at the same time restoring and gaining him requires one who is full of grace. You know you are right, yet you do not stand on your right. You are right, but you are not proud. You are right, but still humble and gentle. You are right, and yet you are able to show your brother that he is wrong. Let me tell you, it requires you to set yourself completely aside before you can tell your brother his fault. If you yourself are involved, you will never be able to fulfill this task.

May brothers and sisters learn this lesson. In allowing your brother to sin against you, the Lord has looked upon you and has chosen you to be a vessel for restoration. You have been given a great burden, and you must not fail. You must not make excuses because of the difficulties involved. To make excuses is a problem of brothers and sisters. To do so may allow corruption to be brought into the life of Christ in the church. The power of the church, the life of the body, the work of the various ministries as well as the strength to grow are often counteracted by the burdens of undealt matters.

Do you see the relationship between the church and undealt matters? Many difficulties in the body of Christ lie here. There are some covered up, unsolved matters. They are not spoken about, yet are always present. After a period of time, they become such a heavy burden that the church can hardly move on. Brothers and sisters, therefore, must learn to alleviate the burden of the church. When anyone sins against you, you are not to shut your eyes but are to deal with it faithfully in a right attitude and spirit. Thus shall you gain your brother. Otherwise the matter will remain in the church. I do hope that new believers will remember especially the words of Matthew 18:15 so that when occasion arises they may know what to do.

2. TAKE ONE OR TWO MORE

Verse 16 tells us what we should do in case we fail to restore a brother in this personal way. "But if he hear thee not, take with thee one or two more, that at the mouth of two witnesses or three every word may be established." After you have gone to him and spoken in a good attitude, with gentle words, out of a right motive, if he still refuse to hear you, then you may tell it to another person. I must be very strict here by saying you should never tell anybody else until your brother has refused to hear you. If two of God's children have trouble between them they can solve it easily by kneeling together before God and humbly forgiving and forgetting.

If news of the problem inadvertently comes to the ear of a third person, the result will be an increase of the sickness. A wound heals when no foreign particles get into it. Telling a third person, though, is like rubbing dirt into an open wound. It simply aggravates the trouble. Broken bones may be joined, but not if things are placed between them. Likewise, in case there is trouble between brothers and sisters, it should be dealt with properly. Only after your personal, private persuasion has failed, can you tell another person. Such telling is not for gossip but for having fellowship.

If you discover that your brother will not accept your word, the Lord says, "Take with thee one or two more." These may be the elders of the church or they may be other brothers. Even at this juncture, you do not tell it to just anybody. You tell it to one or two brothers in the Lord who are well experienced and have spiritual weight. You lay the matter before them and ask their advice. Is it true that this brother is wrong? What do you brothers think about it? After these two brothers have considered the matter prayerfully before God and judged according to their spiritual discernment, they may agree that this brother has indeed done wrong. Now the question is no longer your hurt feelings. You may take these two or three witnesses to the brother and say, "You have done wrong in this matter. It will obstruct your spiritual future. You must repent and acknowledge that you are wrong."

"That at the mouth of two witnesses or three every word may be established." These two or three witnesses cannot be persons who are talkative or who talk carelessly. If they are, they will not be respected and honored. They must be dependable persons with honesty, weight, and experience in the Lord. Every word is then established in the mouths of two or three witnesses.

3. TELL THE CHURCH

The rule of the church is: it is best if you personally can resolve the problem; otherwise you have to seek for a way to purity. If the difficulty is minor, you may simply forgive and forget. But if it affects fellowship, you must learn to deal with it. If you fail in your dealing with it personally, then you can bring in two or three witnesses. "And if he refuse to hear them, tell it unto the church" (v. 17). I think the church here refers to the responsible brothers of the church privately, not at a time when the whole church assembles. You tell the responsible brothers of the difficulty between you and your brother and ask them for advice.

If the church is one about it and if the conscience of the church condemns a brother, he must be wrong. If he is a brother who lives before God, he will set aside his own opinion and accept the testimony of the two or three witnesses. If he refuses to accept their witness, he should at least accept the decision of the church. "Since all the brothers and sisters judge that I am wrong, I must be wrong no matter how right or wrong I think I am." The consensus of the church is the mind of the Lord. The Lord is here in the church; this is His judgment. How we need to learn to be soft and tender when we hear what the church has to say to us. We should not trust our own feeling, nor be confident of ourselves. We ought to accept the feeling of the church.

What should be done if he refuses to hear the church? "And if he refuse to hear the church also, let him be unto thee as the Gentile and the publican" (v. 17). How very serious this word is. It means that all the brothers and sisters in the church will have no fellowship with him. This, in fact, makes him an outsider. Since the difficulty is not resolved, the church looks upon him as a Gentile and a publican; they have no fellowship with him. Every one of us, therefore, must learn to accept the decision of the church.

New believers should see that the word in Matthew 18:18–20 is based on what we have just mentioned. "Truly

I say unto you, what thing soever ye shall bind on earth shall be bound in heaven; and what things soever ye shall loose on earth shall be loosed in heaven" (v. 18). This refers back to the one with whom the church has dealt. Naturally, the scope of this verse covers more than that; still, in the matter before us the church looks upon the one who refuses to hear as a Gentile and a publican. Let us remember that what we bind on earth shall be bound in heaven, and what we loose on earth shall be loosed in heaven. What the church does on earth, the Lord in heaven ratifies. Hence, God's children should learn to accept the decision of the church.

What is said in verses 19 and 20 also follows this line. "Again I say unto you, that if two of you shall agree on earth as touching anything that they shall ask, it shall be done for them of my Father who is in heaven. For where two or three are gathered together in my name, there am I in the midst of them." This refers back to the two or three witnesses and to the church. The church has looked on the offender as a Gentile and a publican. What the church has done, the Lord says he will also do in heaven.

Perhaps some may ask, what is the use of asking two or three to go with you? Remember, the principle of two or three is the principle of the church. If two or three should agree on a certain matter before God, the Lord promises that He will acknowledge it in heaven. The words in Matthew 18:18–20 are derived from the case of dealing with a brother. It is from the two or three to the whole church. I hope brothers and sisters will learn to submit to the decision of the church.

61

What New Believers Should Learn

If anyone sins against you, you should do two things: first, you must exhort or persuade him; second, you must forgive him.

If a person who has sinned against you refuses to acknowledge it even after the church comes to him, the problem continues on. It is not a matter of whether or not you will forgive him (you personally should still forgive him), but that in your outward relationship God says he must be to you as a Gentile. This is better than to let him stay in the church, for difficulty in the church will burden the church. It is better to relieve such pressure.

New believers should learn, as soon as a difficulty arises, to forgive it at once. Many matters will thus be resolved, especially matters of minor consequence. Sometimes, though, the fault is such that you feel it needs to be restored before God; then you should go to your brother and persuade and restore him. If he acknowledges his fault, forgive him, and the matter is solved. If he refuses to listen, we must prayerfully consider it before God and try to solve it properly. Our attitude toward the one who has sinned against us must be good. We are clear that being ourselves recipients of grace we must be gracious toward others. Having been forgiven our debt, we cannot press those who are indebted to us. Let us be careful not to speak inadvertently. Let our motive be forgiving, not faultfinding. If we stand on this ground and act according to God's Word, I trust the church will be saved from many errors. May God be gracious to us.

THE BELIEVER'S REACTION

Ye have heard that it was said, An eye for an eye, and a tooth for a tooth: but I say unto you, Resist not him that is evil: but whosoever smiteth thee on thy right cheek, turn to him the other also. And if any man would go to law with thee, and take away thy coat, let him have thy cloak also. And whosoever shall compel thee to go one mile, go with him two. Give to him that asketh thee, and from him that would borrow of thee turn not thou away.

Ye have heard that it was said, Thou shalt love thy neighbor, and hate thine enemy: but I say unto you, Love your enemies, and pray for them that persecute you; that ye may be sons of your Father who is in heaven: for he maketh his sun to rise on the evil and the good, and sendeth rain on the just and the unjust. For if ye love them that love you, what reward have ye? do not even the publicans the same? And if ye salute your brethren only, what do ye more than others? do not even the Gentiles the same? Ye therefore shall be perfect, as your heavenly Father is perfect.

Matt. 5:38–48

63

At least half, if not more, of our lives are lived in reactions. People talk and we feel happy; this is reaction. They talk and we become angry; this also is reaction. Somebody does a certain thing and we consider it wrong; this is reaction. Someone does something against us, so we lose our temper; this too is reaction. We become irritated when provoked, we defend ourselves when misunderstood, we endure when ill-treated; these all are reactions. In analyzing our lives, it seems that more than half of them are lived in reactions.

Difference in Reaction of Believer and Unbeliever

We Christians also live in reactions, but ours are different from those of the unbelievers. By observing how a person reacts, we can judge who he is. A Christian should not have unchristian reactions, nor can a non-Christian have true Christian reactions. If you want to know what sort of person someone is, just notice the kind of reactions he has.

Believers' reactions should differ from those of other people. The Lord both charges us as to how we should react and gives us the power to do it. He does not want us to react carelessly. Christian life is a chain of reactions. If we react properly, we are good Christians; otherwise we are poor Christians.

After we believe in the Lord and are saved, we are Christians. The Lord has given to us definite commands as to how we must react whenever we are faced with trials and persecutions. We are not given the liberty to react as we please. Christians' reactions, as well as their lives, should be under the control of God. If God controls our reactions, we will not react freely. As He commands us, so will we react. It is His life within us, the life He has given us that does the reacting.

Teaching of the Lord on the Mount

How did people in the Old Testament under the dispensation of the law react? "Ye have heard that it was said, an eye for an eye, and a tooth for a tooth" (Matt. 5:38). This passage is rather simple; it speaks of reactions. If anyone hurts my eye, I will hurt his eye; if anyone breaks my tooth, I will do the same to him. I do something because you have done something—this is reaction. The Old Testament under the law produces this kind of reaction.

New Testament believers, however, have a different kind of reaction. The Lord says, "But I say unto you, resist not him that is evil" (v. 39). Your reaction should be different; you should not resist evil people.

In the following quotation there are three things. These words are famous; many people know them. "But whosoever smiteth thee on thy right cheek, turn to him the other also. And if any man would go to law with thee, and take away thy coat, let him have thy cloak also. And whosoever shall compel thee to go one mile, go with him two" (vv. 39–41). Do you see that the left cheek, the cloak and the second mile are Christian reactions? The right cheek, the coat, and the first mile are man's works. What man demands is the first mile, but the Christian reaction is the second mile. What people ask for is the coat, but we give an additional cloak. What people seek is the right cheek, but we respond with the left cheek as well. This whole passage in Matthew tells us that we Christians ought to have a different kind of reaction.

I hope you know what the Christian reaction is. We should not need to be told this if we have been Christians for many years. It is best if during the first few days of our Christian life, we learn how the Lord wants us to react, for we cannot be good Christians unless we react properly. How can we react against nature, that is, against the life which God has given us, and reach God's standard? Therefore, let our reactions be Christian reactions. We cannot say we are Christian yet react in a worldly manner.

Before we became Christians, we had our reactions. But now we should not react as in former days. We must react as Christians.

"Give to him that asketh thee, and from him that would borrow of thee turn not thou away" (v. 42). These are all reactions. If anyone asks of you, give it to him. If anyone desires to borrow from you, do not turn him away unless you have nothing you can give.

"Ye have heard that it was said, thou shalt love thy neighbor, and hate thy enemy" (v. 43). These are the reactions of those under the law. If you are my neighbor, my reaction is love; but if you are my enemy, my reaction is hate.

"But I say unto you, love your enemies" (v. 44). The Christian reaction is different. He is your enemy, but you love him. "And pray for them that persecute you." He is intent on persecuting me, but my reaction is to pray for him.

"That ye may be sons of your Father who is in heaven: for he maketh his sun to rise on the evil and on the good, and sendeth rain on the just and on the unjust" (v. 45).

These are God's reactions. God makes His sun shine on the evil as well as on the good; He sends rain on the unjust as well as on the just. His reactions remain constant. He has no evil reaction against men.

"For if ye love them that love you, what reward have ye? Do not even the publicans the same?" (v. 46). What reward will you have if you react in love to those who love you? The publicans do the same thing. You are no different from the publicans. Such reaction is too easy, too cheap, too low.

"And if ye salute your brethren only, what do ye more than others? Do not even the Gentiles the same?" (v. 47). He and I are brothers, so I salute him; but if we have something between us, I will not even speak to him. Then am I different from the Gentiles? Such reaction is too low, as low as that of the Gentiles.

"Ye therefore shall be perfect, as your heavenly Father is perfect" (v. 48). This is to say that in the matter of reaction, we must be like God.

Necessity of Solving the Matter of Reaction

Do we see that this passage of Scripture deals exclusively with the Christian reaction? If we solve the matter of reactions, we will solve more than half of our Christian life, for we react more than we act. Only occasionally do we initiate; usually there is an action to which we react in one of any number of ways. Reactions surpass actions in number.

Remember, solving the reaction problem resolves more than half of our Christian life. People act; we react. They say something; we react. They show some kind of attitude;

we react. We are simply full of reactions. Since the greater part of our life is composed of reactions, for us to react in the Christian way is acceptable to God.

Perhaps you would like to ask why we should pay attention to this matter. May I frankly remind you to not consider what we are touching upon as unimportant. For over twenty years, I have had a very heavy feeling within me: many who have been Christians for years still do not know what the Lord demands of them in their reactions. They may have read the teaching of the Lord on the mount dozens of times and been Christians for many, many years, yet fail to see what the Lord requires of their reactions. As a result, after so many years of being Christians, their reactions still are basically wrong. When things happen to them, they argue, they reason, they talk about the law, and they demand righteousness. They have not seen what the Christian reaction is. Instead, they react according to the righteousness of the law, of the Gentiles, and of the publicans. They are just like Gentiles and publicans. They keep saying, "Am I not right?" They feel they are quite reasonable. They forget that Christians should not reason in such things; they do not know what the Christian reaction is. This, indeed, is a big problem.

Even if you have a good reason, you should not speak of it. To take this step is wrong. What you say may or may not be trustworthy, but in saying it you show a wrong attitude. A person who does not know what the Christian way of reaction is may consider himself right in his reactions. According to his thinking, it is all right for people in the church to devour each other. When a brother keeps silence and reacts in a true Christian way, the man who does not know the Christian way of reacting considers such silence a sure sign of being wrong. Thus the church falls into the way of the world.

Therefore new believers must be shown what the Christian reaction is. Then they will know how they should live before God. They will also be able to judge others differently. Otherwise, they misjudge others by justifying those who do not react in the Christian way and condemning those who do live in this way. Recently I was the object of many words; one person said that I was so rebuked I could not say a word. The person who said this thought that it was right to open one's mouth and wrong to keep one's mouth shut. Sorry to say, that person did not know what the cross is nor what it means to react in the Christian way. New believers ought to learn during the first few months that to be a Christian includes having a certain kind of reaction. If they do not react as a Christian, they are the same as the publicans and the Gentiles. A Christian ought to react in the Christian way.

Ordinarily there is little initiative expressed in our life; daily we live in reactions. More than half of our life is passive. We react to how people act to us. We feel as others feel. In view of this, we will not have much of a life before God if our reactions are wrong.

Basic Principle of Reaction

Having briefly gone through our passage in Matthew, we can now discover what the basic principle of the Christian reaction is. Man's reactions to ordinary matters may be divided into three levels: first, the level of reason; second, the level of good conduct; and third, the level of God's life. He who lives on the level of reason will react temperamentally and angrily; he who lives on the level of good conduct will react patiently; but he who lives in God's holy life will react transcendently.

If someone strikes your right cheek, you will say, "Why did you hit me?" Your heart is full of reasoning. Your cheek has been hit, you are angry and thus you reason with the one who did it. You are standing on the level of reason, and your reaction is anger and loss of temper. Or perhaps you are aware of the fact that Christians ought to behave well and that it is wrong for you to get angry. So you react as one whose coat has been taken from him by someone; you bear it with patience; you let them take it without uttering a word. You feel that as a Christian you cannot say anything but should be patient. Such reaction seems to be better than losing your temper. But the Lord tells us there is still another kind of reaction—a reaction which He expects of us.

The reaction which the Lord has ordained for us is not that we get angry when people strike our cheek, nor that we try to be patient when others take our coat. The Lord has not said if people force you to walk one mile, walk that mile patiently. He says, instead, turn your left cheek to him. If he wants your coat, give him also your cloak; or, in modern terms, if he wants your shirt, give him also your coat. If he compels you to walk one mile, go the second mile with him. Such reaction is not called patience but transcendence. It rises above the demands of man. Man only demands so much, but, because we are before God, we give much more than his demand. It is not just being patient but transcending man's demand.

Brothers and sisters, I desire that from the first day of your faith in Christ, you may know what a believer's life is. The Lord has shown us that Christians should have only one reaction. That reaction is neither reasoning nor enduring, but transcending. Remember, if it is not transcendent, it is not Christian. To be patient is insufficient for a Christian. The Lord no longer says, an eye for an eye—if someone hurts my eye, I will hurt his. He says instead, add another eye. If someone hurts my eye, I give him another. Do you see that the Christian reaction is neither revenge in striking back nor patience in enduring? It is to give another eye.

Meaning of Christian Reaction

From the Old Testament's an eye for an eye to the New Testament's an eye plus an eye, from a shirt for a shirt to a shirt with a coat, from a mile for a mile to a mile plus a mile—between these two different kinds of reactions, there are at least two steps. An eye for an eye is one reaction; anger is another reaction; patience is still another reaction; and adding another eye is one more reaction. Of these four reactions, three have to be rejected. By seeing what God requires of us, we know what our reactions ought to be.

Let us explain the three hypothetical cases further. To have one's cheek struck is a disgrace. The Jews took it that way and so did the Romans. In many Roman books we find recorded how oftentimes Roman slaves would rather be killed than have their cheeks struck by their masters. They could bear killing but not having their cheeks struck. To be struck on the cheek was considered at that time as a disgrace of the greatest magnitude.

Clothing is one of man's most legitimate possessions, for men cannot be without clothing. Even the poorest needs to be clothed with shirt and coat. However ascetic people are, they still need to wear a shirt and a coat. This is universally accepted as a most legitimate requirement of life. But today someone wants to take away your shirt. Mind you, he does not want your property or land but your shirt. This touches the most basic of your possessions and the most legitimate of all. In taking your shirt, he has to first make you take off your coat. So it reaches to the depth of your possessions. If smiting the cheek means disgrace, then taking the shirt means touching the depth of man's possessions.

As to being forced to walk one mile, the stress here is on compulsion; it is a matter of the will. I did not intend to go that way, but I was forced to. This hurts my will. I have to suppress my will in order to walk that way.

The Christian reaction is the left cheek, the coat, and the second mile. If people want my shirt, I give also my coat. If they compel me to walk one mile, I go the second mile. If they smite my right cheek, I turn the left cheek. All these show that I am not at all affected by the right cheek, the shirt, or the first mile. Therefore, such reaction is transcendent. If I were touched by the right cheek, I would not offer the left cheek. If I could not stand the first mile, would I walk the second mile? So, the question we must each ask ourselves is, how do I react?

We Christians are being delivered from the senses of disgrace or glory, of material possessions, and of self-will. As we are delivered, we transcend the problems of "face" or pride, of possession, and of self-will. We no longer are affected by these things. We are able to walk the second mile.

We need to learn before God not to reason or argue. The first lesson of the cross is, do not reason. I do not believe that brothers and sisters will fall to such an extent as to seek revenge, so we will not touch upon the reaction of an eye for an eye or a tooth for a tooth. We do, however, realize that it is possible for revenge to be one kind of reaction. We would rather, however, concentrate on the three other reactions. Though I do not believe a brother or sister will fall to the level of the law in seeking revenge, yet I am afraid there are many who will reason and talk about righteousness. "You should not have struck me," you reason. Remember, if anyone reasons with people, it shows he is already touched by the incident. The Lord's reaction is different. He shows us that when people ill-treat us without reason, we can do just the opposite—treat them well without reason. As the first mile is absolutely unreasonable, so is the second mile wholly unreasonable. Both are without reason. To strike the right cheek is to strike with no reason; to offer the left cheek to be struck is also totally without reason. If it is utterly unreasonable for one's shirt to be taken away, it is equally unreasonable to give away the coat. Do you see that Christians are not to reason? If others are unreasonably bad, then we must be unreasonably good!

A Christian does neither the right thing nor the good thing. When someone wants to take away my shirt, it is right for me not to give it to him, but it would be good if I did. However, as a Christian, I go further; I give both the shirt and the coat to him. Our way is clear. It is right for me not to give him my shirt. Why should I give it to him just because he wants to take it away from me? Nonetheless, it is good of me if I do give it to him; this is what a good person would do. But, remember, you are not a Christian because you do the right thing, nor are you a

Christian because you do the good thing. A Christian gives not only the shirt but the coat as well. He who gives the second garment is a Christian.

What, then, is the Christian reaction? The Christian reaction is not to do the right thing nor the good thing but the transcendent thing. The more a child of God is persecuted and pressed and frustrated, the higher he climbs. How pitiful if you fall the moment you are squeezed. It is really regretful to lose your temper, to argue, or even to endure. The time when you are severely pressed against the wall is the time for you to rise up. Let me tell you, this is what a Christian is.

I remember a brother who passed away many years ago. I particularly remember one comment made about him: If you had never been his enemy, you would never know how great was his love. This truly is a good word. It ought to be true of every Christian. The more fiercely he is persecuted, the greater is his power. The worse he is treated, the greater he becomes. When the brother just mentioned died, many brethren gave this observation: "To know the strength of his love required being his fiercest enemy. We never treated him badly enough, for the worse we were, the greater his love was." This is what we call the Christian reaction. The more you block his way, the wider the road opens up to him.

Do remember that this is not something too profound. Matthew 5 through 7 records the first sermon of the Lord Jesus. The teaching on the mount was the first the disciples heard. Likewise, it is the teaching we should first give to new believers. As soon as people come in, they should be told what the Christian reaction is. To be Christian is to react in such-and-such a way. If you do not react so, let me tell you, you will not feel comfortable within. If a Christian reasons with people, he will feel ill at ease when he returns home. If he murmurs when something is taken away from him, he will not feel comfortable when he gets home. But when someone takes his shirt and he gives also his coat, he will feel so happy that he will want to shout, "Hallelujah." Is it not so? If you hold on to things, you feel uncomfortable. If you refuse to lend when asked, you save the money but you also sacrifice your joy. Give to him who asks of you. And if any man would go to court to take away your shirt, give him also your coat. To be Christian in this way will fill you with joy.

Many Christians have sad faces because they refuse to go the second mile. Because of refusing, their hearts can no longer sing. Were they to go the second mile, they would feel so relieved that they could sing aloud for joy.

Many brothers and sisters have trouble with their reactions because they do not know the Lord. They worry about walking the second mile, turning the left cheek and giving away their coat. They keep on saying how unreasonable it is. But let me tell you frankly, it is the Lord who says, "Turn to him the other also." The second mile, the coat, and the left cheek are the Lord's demands, not man's. All who have trouble with the second garment, the other cheek, and the second mile have trouble with the Lord, not with man.

The Lord's command is stricter than the demand of unreasonable people. If you think that man is unreasonable, remember that the Lord is much more unreasonable. If the first garment is unreasonable, the second garment is even more unreasonable. If one cheek should not be smitten, even more so the other one should not be. If one mile is unreasonable, the second mile is more unreasonable. But the second one is the Lord's requirement, the

Lord's command. So His command is stricter than the demand of an unreasonable man.

Why is the command of the Lord so strict? Because He knows that the life which He gives us is a transcendent life. This life will never be comfortable if it does not transcend. It will not be happy unless it transcends. The more it is subject to disgrace, loss, or difficulty, the greater is the manifestation of its power.

So this is the Christian way of reacting. Such a life, brethren, is transcendent, climbing high. It is the believer's way of living. Anything less is unchristian.

Shall I tell you that some people are so ignorant of the Bible that they take the teaching on the mount in Matthew 5 through 7 as the law? No, this is not law; this is grace. I trust you all know what grace is. Grace is giving what is undeserved. Let me tell you, the first cheek, the first garment, and the first mile are already grace. An eye for an eye is law; a tooth for a tooth is law. The right cheek is already grace, so is the shirt, and so is the first mile. All these are undeserved. But the life within us so transcends these things that they cannot touch us. Because of this transcendent life, not only can we walk the first mile but also we must walk the second mile. We will give not only the shirt but also the coat. We will turn our left cheek as well as our right cheek. Let me say, this is grace upon grace. This is not God's grace, but the grace of God's children. This is not law, but the grace of the children of God. This is God's children doing things according to the God of grace. As God gives people what they do not deserve, so we give them more than they ask for. Do you see this is what it means to be a Christian?

Why do things which are beyond man? Because the teaching on the mount has enlarged our capacity. God enlarges us through these reactions. Many things are precious to us. But when not only the shirt but also the coat goes and when this happens again and again, we then become bigger and bigger. We will be many times bigger than our coat; we will be much, much bigger than our shirt. Many Christians are as tight as the garments they wear. Ill-treatment of just one precious garment touches them, causing them to lose their temper and to lose their Christian dignity. Is a garment worth striving for at the cost of Christian dignity? But, alas, we find such small people everywhere.

God has given you a big life; therefore, it is possible for you to be constantly enlarged. Not only can one garment go, so can a hundred garments. If you can walk the first mile when compelled, you can also walk the second mile voluntarily. Thus you will be enlarged by God. Man's pride is extremely important. He cannot stand shame and disgrace. Many are willing to part with their garments, but they cannot bear disgrace. They find it hard even to take a few contemptuous words. But here you are: you not only endure patiently but even will gladly be smitten. As you turn the left cheek, you grow. It is by doing these undeserved things to others that you grow and keep on growing.

Your will is strong; you always insist on doing things a certain way. Today you are pressed to the point that you are willing to add obedience; you are willing to walk the second mile. Let me tell you, when your will is unbent, such pressure is exceedingly painful. If you are forced to bend, you suffer. But if you willingly bend your will, you then can grow by leaps and bounds.

During these days, I continuously meet small people in the world. But also during these days, I have *not* met many big people in the church. It is my hope that new believers will walk this road of reacting in God's way; thus they will grow. We grow by reacting in the right way. Reacting transcendently by the life of God is the basic law of growth. If we are able to react always according to this transcendent life, we will become bigger and bigger. No material thing will hold us; no disgrace or contempt will frustrate us; not even our own strong will can limit us. We just keep on growing. If it is not so, the church will be filled with small people.

Transcendent Life Demanded

In the world you sometimes may see big people, or, at least, people who appear to be big. Some people have especially good tempers; they do not reason when beaten. Others are so timid that they do not say anything because they are afraid, but I dare say that in their hearts they are full of annoyance. Their reactions are as small as their lives. Thus I cannot say that the second mile is enough in itself, for the second mile is a principle—the principle of transcendency. The left cheek is also a principle—the same principle, the principle of transcendency. Only reactions that stem from this principle are good enough for the Christian.

Transcendency means you rise above the situation. You do not just bite your teeth and let someone strike you. You do not just reluctantly give your shirt to him who asks for it. You do not just warily walk a mile because compelled to do so. To do any of these is useless, for you have not transcended. Who, then, can transcend? It is he to whom the Lord has given a life so rich that when disgraced he can turn the left cheek. It is he who has a life so big that he can walk the second mile when only compelled to walk one mile. In other words, Christian reaction is neither forced nor meager.

I heard a sister say, "I nearly lost my temper." When she said it, she looked as if she were victorious. But let me tell you, this is not the Christian reaction; genuine Christian reaction must be abundant, with more to spare. You must be able to stand more. This is called the second mile. If you bear someone treating you badly, this is the right cheek. But if you treat him doubly well in return, you are more than a conqueror before God; this is the left cheek. The left cheek means fulness; it means having more to spare. Let me say again, Christian victory is always running over; it is never barely enough. A Christian has more than enough to spare. He always transcends what he himself can do. So his victory is not forced. He does not need to bite his teeth and reason in order to preserve himself. He overcomes easily before the Lord. He allows the Lord to enlarge him time and time again. He is always able to manifest the grace of the children of God.

Why must we turn the left cheek? To do so indicates that when the Lord permits man's hand to ill-treat us, our choice is to let the Lord increase His work in us rather than to lessen it. Hence, we turn the left cheek. By means of a human hand, the Lord intends to increase our capacity and make us grow. That human hand works only on the right cheek, but we add the left cheek. So our reaction not only does not resist what the Lord is doing through man, but also allows Him to increase His work. The Lord deals with us; so then we also deal with ourselves. In other words, when people smite our right cheek, we seem to join hands with them to smite ourselves. We do not stand in opposition to those who smite us;

instead we stand on their side. We feel one stroke is not enough, so we add another stroke.

Our prayer is, "May the Lord's hand be on me. If I lose all, I will not be able to lose any more. When I am totally dead, I will not be able to die further. As long as I may yet die, I have not died enough. Since I may still lose, I have not lost enough. I am willing to increase the Lord's hand on me, rather than to lighten it." If we are able to stand on the Lord's side and deal with ourselves, we will never entertain the thought of revenge on others.

Our transcendency is before the Lord for no one demands more than the Lord. The most people can demand is only one mile, but what the Lord requires is the second mile. Do you see how strict this is? What man may compel me to do is limited to the first mile, but what I give him is something more. I add to it, for my transcendency is with the Lord.

Christian Ground Firmly Taken

Which is better—to smite or to be smitten? Do you admire the way of most people? Because they smite others, would you do the same? Let me tell you, he who smites others is not acting as a Christian.

If you are struck by a brother today, do you know what he is giving you? He is giving you a great opportunity— one which cannot be better—to be enlarged as a Christian. Suppose your reaction is: how dare that brother hit me? How unreasonable he is! If your reaction is that, will you not then be tempted to strike back? Such a reaction is unchristian. When that brother smites you, you know immediately that he is not acting as a Christian, but at the same time you also realize that he has given you a fine opportunity to react like one.

All who smite others have lost their Christian dignity. Let us not admire them. But let us also remember that each time people ill-treat us, speak evilly of us, or make unreasonable demands of us, they are giving us opportunity to react as Christians. It is as if they are saying: I am not going to be Christian in action, but I will let you!

If a brother should sue you in court and try to take away money or clothing from you, he is telling you that he is no longer acting as a Christian but that he will let you do so. He forfeits his Christian ground but puts you on that ground. Should you not, then, thank God for the opportunity? You should say, "O God, I thank You and I praise You, because You put me on Christian ground. This, indeed, is Your grace." If you fall to the level of hitting back, you are finished. You lose your Christian ground and give others that opportunity. Therefore, brothers and sisters should strive to stand on Christian ground.

Once I had a certain transaction with a brother. I owed him nothing but he asked me for a large sum of money. I forget the exact amount, probably it was sixty-eight thousand dollars. My first reaction was that of irritation. How could he be a Christian and be so unreasonable? This was really too low. Could a righteous person make such a demand? But a second reaction came to me. I was happy; I was happy to give to him even though he was wrong. So I asked him, "Brother, do you really want the money?" He answered, "I do." It was at that time that the Lord gave me the word, "He is giving you an opportunity to be an enlarged Christian." This was the first time the Lord spoke this to me. Consequently, I prepared the money and gave it to him.

Since that day I have learned a lesson. When people act like that brother, they withdraw themselves from Christian ground, yet they give us an opportunity to be on that ground. If, under such circumstances, we too withdraw from Christian ground, it is most shameful and pitiable. We need to learn to say, "The Lord has put us on this ground that we may have the opportunity to be Christian in action." We will tell the Lord, "Lord, I want to act like a Christian." No loss can be greater than not being Christian in action. To be smitten is a great loss; to be deprived of things is a great loss; to suffer disgrace is a great loss; to lose freedom is a great loss. But may I tell you, in allowing these things the Lord shows His confidence in you, wanting you to manifest His grace. You are to manifest not merely His power but also His grace and His generosity toward people. If we fail in this, how very great is the loss.

People may think it is the strong who smite others; but I say the strong is able to be smitten and not strike back. He who is unable to control his temper is weak; but he who can restrain himself is strong. The smitten one is the strong one; the one who turns his left cheek is really strong. He is strong because he can turn his left cheek and smite himself. Let us learn to know what is of spiritual value before God, not just of worldly value. Do not live by worldly standards, but live by spiritual standards.

I therefore desire all new believers to know what the Christian reaction is. Do not wait for three, five, eight, or ten years before you get on the road. Do not take the teaching on the mount as something profound. No Christian ought to delay learning the teaching on the mount. He should learn it as soon as he believes in the Lord, for the teaching on the mount is the first teaching. It stands right at the front door; it is not something that you see after having gone on with the Lord for some years. The teaching on the mount is the Christian's basic reaction; it is a reaction according to Christian nature. No spiritual progress is required to have this reaction. As soon as you believe in the Lord Jesus, you have such reactions. You will naturally have this experience. When you walk the second mile, your heart is joyful. Only by so doing are you comfortable and happy within. This life needs persecution, disgrace, and ill-treatment. The greater the pressure, the stronger is the power of the manifestation of God's life.

Two Things Concerning the Reaction of Life

Finally, concerning this life there are two things worth special notice.

1. PRAY DAILY TO NOT BE BROUGHT INTO TEMPTATION

First of all, we need to pray daily that the Lord not bring us into temptation but deliver us from the evil one. Having a life principle such as this, we are unable, according to the world's estimate, to live at all. The reaction which the Lord has given us is something impossible on earth. After a few attempts on our own, all the resources we have will be gone. For this reason, the Lord inserts such a prayer in the teaching on the mount. "And bring us not into temptation, but deliver us from the evil one" (Matt. 6:13). Only by the Lord's protection are we able to live in this world. Without His protection, we cannot live a day. Hence, this prayer is a must. It would not matter if we did not live such a life nor have such a reaction. But if we do live by the life of God, then we have to pray this prayer daily.

The principle of the Christian life must not be told to unbelievers, nor should it be told to nominal Christians. In the following chapter in Matthew, we find it is said: "Give not that which is holy unto the dogs, neither cast your pearls before the swine, lest haply they trample them under their feet, and turn and rend you" (Matt. 7:6). Both dogs and swine are unclean. Dogs stand for all that is wicked and dirty. Swine represent lifeless Christians—outwardly they are cloven-footed and parted in hoof but inwardly they do not chew the cud. Thus, outwardly they are Christians, but inwardly they are not. Swine in the Bible stand for nominal Christians. These words should not be spoken to them or to unbelievers because to do so is to court trouble. They will bite us or challenge us with, "Turn your cheek and see." Let us pray that we may be saved from these troubles.

2. KEEP THE PROPER CHRISTIAN REACTION

We do not seek for trouble. However, if under God's permission or arrangement or control of the Holy Spirit, we are faced with such a situation, whether it comes from unbelievers or from believers, we must not draw back. We must maintain a proper reaction.

I believe the words we have said are sufficient. A Christian life is surprising. The more you are persecuted, troubled, and unreasonably treated, the happier you are before God. This alone is the way of happiness. Will you try it out? If you smite a person, will you feel comfortable or uncomfortable? It is better if you are smitten. If I were to smite a brother and he immediately turned the other cheek to me, I would be uncomfortable for a whole month.

As a Christian, do not live on earth taking advantage of people. If you take people's advantage, you will at least lose a month before God, for you will not be able to rise up spiritually. Taking advantage on earth is not worth it. It is better to be beaten; then you will sleep well, eat well, sing well. Do not even think that taking advantage is really advantageous. I trust that if we react aright, we will walk aright. This is a basic life principle which must not be overlooked.

DELIVERANCE

For that which I do I know not; for not what I would, that
do I practise; but what I hate, that I do. But if what I
would not, that I do, I consent unto the law that it is good.
So now it is no more I that do it, but sin which dwelleth in
me. For I know that in me, that is, in my flesh, dwelleth no
good thing: for to will is present with me, but to do that
which is good is not. For the good which I would I do not;
but the evil which I would not, that I practise. But if what I
would not, that I do, it is no more I that do it, but sin
which dwelleth in me. I find then the law, that, to me who
would do good, evil is present. For I delight in the law of
God after the inward man: but I see a different law in my
members, warring against the law of my mind, and
bringing me into captivity under the law of sin which is in
my members. Wretched man that I am! who shall deliver
me out of the body of this death? I thank God through
Jesus Christ our Lord. So then I of myself with the mind,
indeed, serve the law of God; but with the flesh the law of
sin. There is therefore now no condemnation to them that
are in Christ Jesus. For the law of the Spirit of life in Christ
Jesus made me free from the law of sin and death.

Romans 7:15–8:2

The Desire for Deliverance
from Sin

A person who believes in the Lord may immediately be delivered from sin. This experience, however, is not necessarily shared by all new believers. Many are not delivered from sin after they first trust in the Lord. Instead, they often find themselves falling into sin. There is no question at all that they have been saved, that they belong to the Lord and have eternal life. Yet the great difficulty remains that they are frequently disturbed by sin. Because of this, they are unable to serve the Lord as they would like.

It is most painful for a saved person to be disturbed by his continuing sins. Since he is enlightened by God, his conscience is sensitive. In him is the life which condemns sins; so he has the consciousness of sin. He deeply feels his corruption and he abhors himself. This is really an exceedingly painful experience.

Out of this experience comes a problem: many believers do not really know what sin is. Some believers say that sin can be avoided by resisting it. Thus they exert all their strength to resist the temptation to sin. Others contend that sin needs to be overcome. Hence they fight with sin all the time, hoping that they may overcome it. Still others declare that since sin has bound us and robbed us of our freedom, we may be delivered from its enticement if we really struggle hard. Therefore, they do their best to struggle. But these three ideas are only men's thoughts; they are neither God's Word nor God's teaching. None of them can succeed in bringing people to victory.

I hope you will take special note of this matter. I personally believe that as soon as people believe in the

Lord they should be shown the way of deliverance. I do not agree that they must turn many corners before they can be delivered. They should walk this way of freedom from the beginning of their Christian life.

The Word of God does not tell us that we should overcome sin; it does tell us, instead, that we must be delivered from sin, freed from sin. These are the words of the Bible. Sin is a power which holds people. We are to be delivered from its grip, not to destroy its power. We cannot put it to death, but the Lord has removed us from it.

The Law of Sin

For that which I do I know not: for not what I would, that do I practise; but what I hate, that I do. . . . for to will is present with me, but to do that which is good is not. For the good which I would I do not: but the evil which I would not, that I practise. But if what I would not, that I do, it is no more I that do it . . . I find then the law, that, to me who would do good, evil is present. For I delight in the law of God after the inward man: but I see a different law in my members, warring against the law of my mind, and bringing me into captivity under the law of sin which is in my members . . . So then I of myself with the mind, indeed, serve the law of God; but with the flesh the law of sin.

Rom. 7:15–25

You need to find the key to Romans 7. In verses 15 through 20, such words as these are used: "I would," "I would not," "I hate," "to will is present with me," "the good which I would," "the evil which I would not," and so forth. The thoughts constantly repeated are "would," "would not," or "will." But verses 21 through 25 show us

89

another point. The emphasis is no longer "would" or "would not," but is repeatedly seen in words like "the law," "a different law in my members," "into captivity under the law of sin which is in my members," "I of myself with the mind serve the law of God; but with the flesh the law of sin." If you keep these two points of emphases before you, you will be able to solve the problem.

In this section of Romans 7, Paul is thinking of overcoming. He thinks it would be best if he could sin no more and please God by doing that which God can accept. He does not want to sin nor does he like to be defeated. Yet he acknowledges that to will is present with him but to do that which is good is beyond him. He wills to do good, but he cannot do it. Though he tries not to sin, he still does sin. He delights in the law of God, yet he is unable to practice it. In other words, he cannot do what he would do.

In verses 15 through 20, though Paul wills to overcome, yet he suffers total defeat. This shows that the way of victory does not lie in "would" or "would not." Victory is not to be found through man's will. Paul wills and wills, but he ends up in defeat. Therefore, do not think that everything will be all right if only you have the will to do good. To will is with you, but to do is not. All you can do is to will; there is not much use in it.

However, after verse 21 Paul himself finds out why his will to do good is unsuccessful. The reason is that sin is a law. Since sin is a law, it is futile to will. Paul shows us the reason for his defeat. He explains that though he would do good, evil is present with him. He delights in the law of God after the inward man, but with the flesh he serves the law of sin. Whenever he decides to delight in God's law, a different law in his members—the law of sin—brings him into captivity. Any time he wills to do good, evil is present. This is a law.

Many who have been Christians for years still do not see that sin is a power which seems to be quite authoritative. They do not see sin as a law. I hope newly saved brothers and sisters will see this: sin in human experience, as well as in the Bible, is a law. It is not only an influence, a power, but it is also a law. Paul discovered how useless it was for his will to battle against a law.

The Inability of the Will to Overcome the Law

Will is the inner power of man, while law is a natural power. Both are powers. I like to use an illustration to help people understand this matter of law. We know that the earth exerts a gravitational force. This force of gravity is a law. Why do we call it a law? Because it is always so. That which is not incidental is a law. That which is occasional is an historical accident, not a law.

Why is earth's gravitation a law? If I drop my handkerchief, it goes downward. It happens in Shanghai as well as in Foochow. Wherever the handkerchief is dropped, the same thing happens. Gravity pulls it down, so this is called the law of gravitation. Not only is gravity a force; it also is a law. If the handkerchief is only occasionally pulled to the earth, then this force could not be reckoned as a law. A law is something which always acts in the same way. If I throw my Bible upward, it will fall down. If I throw a chair up, it too will fall down. If I jump upward, I will also come down. No matter where or what, what goes up will come down. Then I realize that not only is there a gravitational force exerted by the earth, but there is also a law of gravity.

A law simply means it is always so. It permits no exception. If something happens once one way and another time a different way, it is a matter of history. But if something always happens the same way, it is a law. If a person commits a crime on the street, he will be taken into custody by the police. Should he commit this crime at home, he still will be taken into custody. Whoever murders, regardless of whom or where he murders, he will be taken by the police. This we call a law. A law applies to every person; there are no exceptions. If a man kills someone today, he is taken into custody by the police. But if he kills someone tomorrow and is not taken, kills again the day after tomorrow and is taken, then the matter of taking people into custody cannot be considered a law. A law needs to be consistent. It must be the same yesterday, today, and even tomorrow. The term "law" implies that it continues unchanged.

Every law has its natural power—something not manufactured by human effort. We may use the earth's gravitation as an example. Wherever I drop something, that thing gravitates downward. I do not need to press it down for there is a natural force which causes it to go down. Behind the law is the natural power.

What, then, is the will? Will is man's determination, man's decision. It speaks of what man decides or desires or wills. The exercise of the will is not without its power. If I decide to do a certain thing, I start out to do it. If I decide to walk, I walk; if I decide to eat, I eat. As a person I have a will, and my will produces a power.

However, the power of the will and the power of a law

are different. While the power of the law is natural power, the power of the will is human. Gravitational force does not need the installation of some electrical appliance behind it in order to attract things downward; it acts naturally. If you light a lamp, the heat will naturally rush upward; this too is a law. When air is heated, it rises and expands; this is a law. In rising and expanding, it demonstrates a power, but this power is natural power. The power of the will, however, is something of man. Only that which is living has a will. Neither a chair nor a table has a will of its own. God has a will; man has a will. Only a living being has will. Though man's will does possess some power, it is nonetheless a human power. It is in direct contrast to the power of a law which is a natural power.

The question before us is: when the will and the law are in conflict, which will emerge as conqueror? Usually the will overcomes in the beginning, but the law conquers in the end. Man first overcomes, but the law eventually emerges as victor. For example: I am now holding up a Bible which weighs about half a pound. The force of earth's gravity is operating on this book and is trying its best to pull the Bible to the ground. So the law is working. But I as a person have a will. My hand is lifting the Bible and I will not allow it to fall. I succeed in holding it up; I have overcome. My will is stronger than the law.

Right now, at 8:17 in the evening, I have overcome. But wait till 9:17, and I will start to sigh that my hand will not listen to me. By tomorrow morning at 8:17, I will have to get a doctor to treat me! A law never tires, but my hand does. Man's power cannot overcome natural law. The law of gravitation continues to pull; it pulls without will or thought. I will not let the Bible fall; I forcibly hold onto it. Still the time will come when I can no longer hold on.

When I cease to lift up the Bible, it will drop to the ground. The law works twenty-four hours a day, but I cannot.

Eventually the will of men will be defeated and the law will overcome. All of men's wills cannot conquer natural law. Human will may strenuously resist natural law and may at the beginning seem to overcome, but finally it will have to give in to the law. Do not despise the law of earth's gravitation. You are battling with it daily. All who are now in their graves, if able to speak, would have to concede that they are not as strong as the law. For decades you appear to be daily in ascendancy over gravity. You almost forget the great power of earth's gravity; you live as if there were no death. You are active from morning till night. But there will come a day when you too will be pulled down by the law of sin and death. At that moment, your activity will come to an end. There is nothing you can do; the law has conquered. Can you imagine a person who by force of will could hold onto a Bible so that it never falls? It is impossible. Sooner or later he has to yield; the law will come forth as conqueror.

In Romans 7 the subject is the contrast between law and will. Its theme is very simple, for it deals only with the conflict between will and law. At an earlier time, Paul was not conscious that sin is a law. Paul is the first one in the Bible to discover this truth. He is also first to use the term "law." People know that gravitation is a law, that heat expansion is also a law, but they do not know that sin is a law. At first even Paul did not know this; only after repeatedly sinning did he discover that there was a power in his body which gravitated him to sin. He did not sin purposely, but the power in his body pulled him to sin.

Sinning is more than historical; it is a law. When

temptation comes, we try to resist, but before long we fail; this is our history of defeat. Again temptation comes and again we resist and fail. This happens the tenth time, the hundredth time, the millionth time. It is the same story: temptation comes, we resist; and before we realize it, we are defeated. As this occurs time after time, we begin to see that this is not just an historical fact. It has become a law. Sinning is a law. If one were to sin only once, he might consider it an historical event; however, we cannot say sinning is historical for it is not limited to once. It has become a law.

Temptation comes and I am defeated. I have no way to overcome. Each time it comes, I fail; thus I come to realize that my defeat is more than just defeat; it is the law of defeat in me. Defeat has become a law to me. Brethren, have you seen this? Paul saw it. In verse 21 he tells us his great revelation—a revelation about himself. He says, "I find then the law." This is the first time he realizes it that way. He senses a law. What is it? "That to me who would do good, evil is present." Whenever he wants to do good, he finds evil is present in him. This is the law. When I would do good, sin is present. Sin follows closely after good. Not just once, not just a thousand times, but it is always this way. I now understand it to be a law.

A GREAT REVELATION

It is not that I sin accidentally or occasionally; it is not that I sometimes sin and sometimes do not; sinning is a law to me, for I constantly sin. Because this occurs all the time, I know it is a law. Whenever I would do good, evil is present. When Paul's eyes were opened to this, he realized that all his own efforts were futile. What had he tried? He had tried to do good. He had thought his will could overcome sin, not knowing that no will can ever overcome sin. But as soon as he saw sin as a law, not just a conduct, he immediately conceded that to will was useless. The will could never conquer the law. This, indeed, was a great discovery, a very great revelation.

When through God's mercy anyone is brought to see that sin is a law, he instantly knows how ineffective any method of overcoming sin with the will must be. Before he sees this, he is always making resolutions. When tempted, he bites his teeth and determines to overcome, but eventually he fails. The second time he is tempted he surmises that his first resolution was not strong enough, so this time he makes a firmer resolution to not sin again for any reason. But let me tell you, however strong his resolution is, he still fails again. He may yet conclude that something is wanting in his resolution, so when again tempted, he once more resolves before God and asks the Lord to help him. Since he is not sure of his resolution, he prays, "O Lord, please have mercy on me. Help me that I may not sin this time." After he gets up from his knees, he once again fails. He wonders why he cannot overcome sin by making resolutions. The answer is that it is because no amount of will effort can ever conquer a law.

This hand of mine may be quite strong; it may be able to lift fifty pounds. I have a watch here which weighs only five ounces. It should not be difficult for a hand that can lift fifty pounds to hold up this five-ounce watch. However, there is also a law here exerting its gravitational force on my hand. It pulls every second, every minute, and every hour. It keeps on pulling till I cannot hold this five-ounce watch. The hardship in bearing a load is that the longer you bear it, the heavier the object seems to become—not that the load itself has been increased, but that the law begins to overcome the bearer. The law overcomes the man. Nature overcomes man. This power operates so constantly that it incapacitates you.

Another illustration is losing the temper. This is a common and easily recognized sin. Everyone has committed this sin several times. When you hear some unpleasant words, you feel uncomfortable, as if churning inside. If the same person says more unpleasant words, you may answer in kind. But should he continue to say such unkind words, you may be so stirred that you scold him and beat the table. You have lost your temper. You feel badly afterward because as a Christian you should not lose your temper. So you resolve that next time you will not. You are quite sure you will not. After prayer, you believe you are forgiven. Your heart is full of joy, for you say you will not lose your temper again. But later on, you again hear people say distasteful words. How uncomfortable you feel. You hear further words a second time, and your insides churn like a machine. The third time, you burst. You are, of course, conscious of your fault. How can a Christian lose his temper? You ask the Lord to forgive your sin, and you promise that hereafter you will not lose your temper. But after some time, the experience is repeated all over again. What, then, do you call this? It is not just sinning; it is the law of sin.

Sinning is not accidental; it is a law. If a person kills another person, this is sin. But if he kills every day, this is the law of killing. If a man loses his temper daily, his bad temper has become a law to him. It is not by chance that people sin, nor do they sin only once. People sin countless times throughout their lives. The liars in the world keep on lying; the unclean keep on being unclean; the adulterers keep on committing adultery; the stealers keep on stealing; the ill-tempered keep on losing their temper. It is a law within men which cannot be conquered.

It is a great discovery when the Lord has mercy on you and opens your eyes to see that sin is, indeed, a law. If you see this, victory is not far away. Should you consider sin merely a matter of conduct, you will no doubt try to pray more and to resist more in order to overcome the next time. But it is futile. As the power of sin is strong and constant, so our strength is weak and untrustworthy. As the power of sin is always triumphant, so our power is always yielding. Sin's power is victorious and our power is defeated. The victory of sin is a law, even as our defeat is a law. When I would do good, evil is present. Paul says he has found this to be a law, an unconquerable law.

I do hope that you will be clear on the nature of sin. If you see this law, you will be delivered from many hardships and sorrows. If you are willing to accept God's Word, you will know that sin is a law and that you cannot overcome it with your will. Then you will be able to see the real way to victory. It is a great blessing to find this law. It may take many defeats, possibly hundreds or thousands of defeats, to discover for yourself this law of defeat. You have to be so utterly defeated that one day you realize you can never overcome sin by your will. Sooner or later, sin will rise up and declare that it is a law, so what can you do? Let me tell you, all who trust in their own willpower will have to acknowledge that they can do nothing about it. Since sin is a law, what can you do? You cannot resist it; the power of your will can never overcome the power of a law.

The Way of Victory

We know man is not delivered by exercising his will. When he is using his willpower, he is unable to trust God's way of deliverance. He has to wait for the day when he submits himself to God and confesses that he is utterly undone. Then he will pray, "Lord, I am not going to try again." Whenever one has no way but still thinks of finding a way, he will draw upon his will to help. It is only when he acknowledges he has no way and is not going to find a way that he forsakes calling upon his will for help. Then he will begin to see how to get real deliverance. Then he will read Romans 8.

Brothers and sisters, do not despise Romans 7. Many believers are unable to get out of that chapter. Romans 7 captures more Christians than any other passage in the Bible. Many Christians keep their address in Romans 7! That is where they may be found, for they dwell there. It is useless to preach Romans 8 alone. The question is not whether you know the teaching of Romans 8, but whether you have come out of Romans 7. Many preach on Romans 8 but are still buried in Romans 7. They are yet trying to deal with the law by the power of their will. They are still being defeated. Because they fail to see that sin is a law and that the will cannot overcome the law, they are imprisoned in Romans 7 and cannot enter Romans 8.

New believers should accept what the Word of God says. If you have to wait to find out for yourself, you may have to commit many sins. Even after sinning repeatedly, your eyes still may not be opened. You will have to come to the point where you see that all your battles are futile. Paul said in Romans 7 that it is useless to battle, for who can overcome a law? Thus, at the start of Romans 8 he says, "There is therefore now no condemnation to them that are in Christ Jesus. For the law of the Spirit of life in Christ Jesus made me free from the law of sin and of death" (vv. 1–2). You have seen that sin is a law. You have also seen that it is not possible for man's will to overcome that law. Where, then, is the way of victory, the way of deliverance?

The way of victory is here: "There is therefore now *no condemnation* to them that are in Christ Jesus." The word "condemnation" in the original Greek has two different usages, one legal and the other civil. If the word is used legally, it means "condemnation" as found in the English translation. But in its civil usage, the word means "disabling" or "handicap." According to the context of this passage of Scripture, probably the civil usage is clearer.

We are no longer disabled. Why? Because the Lord Jesus Christ has given us deliverance. It is something the Lord has done. But how does He do it? It is very simple, for it is explained by the second verse: "For the law of the Spirit of life in Christ Jesus made me free from the law of sin and of death." This is the way of victory. Can you alter Romans 8:2 and read it this way: "The Spirit of life in Christ Jesus made me free from sin and death"? I suppose ten Christians out of ten would read the verse this way. But what does it say? It says that "the *law* of the Spirit of life in Christ Jesus made me free from the *law* of sin and of death." Many have seen only the Spirit of life setting them free from sin and death, but have failed to see that it is the *law* of the Spirit of life which sets them free from the *law* of sin and of death.

To learn the lesson that sin and death is a law may take years. But even as it may take a great deal of time and resolution and failure to realize that sin is a law, so it may take years for many believers to discover that the Spirit of life is also a law. Sin has followed us for years and we have had a close association with it; yet we still do not know that it is a law. Likewise, we may have believed in the Lord for many, many years and have known the Holy Spirit in our lives, yet not known Him as a law.

It is a day of great discovery when our eyes are opened by the Lord to see that sin is a law. It is a day of even greater discovery when we are given the revelation that the Holy Spirit is also a law. Only a law can overcome another law. The will cannot overcome the law, but a higher law can overcome a lower law. We can never overcome the law of sin by our human will, but the law of the Spirit of life can set us free from the law of sin and of death.

We know that earth's gravity is a law which holds us. We know too that there is a thing called density. If the density of a thing is exceedingly low, such as in the case of hydrogen, then earth's gravitational force cannot hold it down. By pumping hydrogen into a balloon, we can make the balloon rise. The law of earth's gravitational force is a fixed law, but it only operates within a certain range or degree of density. If the density is too low, the law of gravity does not apply. Then another law takes over, even the law of buoyancy, which sends things upward. This upward surge needs no hand to push, no fan to stir. You just let go, and up it ascends. This law overcomes the other law. It is equally effortless. In a similar manner, the law of the Holy Spirit overcomes the law of sin.

Let us say it another way. To see sin as a law is a big thing, for it makes you decide against battling sin with your willpower. Likewise, seeing the law of the Holy Spirit in your life is another big crisis. Many seem to understand how the Spirit of life gives them life, but have yet to learn that the Holy Spirit in them, that is, the life which God has given them through Jesus Christ, is also a law. If you let this law operate, it will naturally deliver you from the law of sin and of death. When this law delivers you from the other law, it does not require an ounce of your strength. You need not make one resolution, spend any time, nor even lay hold of the Holy Spirit.

May I ask, does anybody need to hold onto the earth's gravitational force? Does someone need to pray that this force will quickly pull things down? No, there is no need to pray, for the earth most spontaneously attracts things downward. It is a law. All one needs to do is to remove his hand, to not purposely hold onto things. When the will is not working, then the law is manifested. When the will is not interfering, the law operates. In a similar way, the Spirit of the Lord in us does not need our help. If you are afraid that the Spirit of the Lord in you may not be responsible and so you rush to help when temptation comes, it shows that you have not seen that the Spirit of the Lord in you is a law.

May new believers see that the Holy Spirit in them is a spontaneous law. If anyone is to be delivered from sin, he has to come to that deliverance naturally. Should he try to get deliverance by exercising his willpower, he will again be defeated. But now those who are in Christ Jesus are no longer handicapped, for the law of the Spirit of life in Christ Jesus has made them free from the law of sin and of death. It is all so simple and so natural. We have been given another law which naturally delivers us from the law of sin and of death.

Someone may ask how this comes about. I do not know, but have you not had some such experience? For example:

someone comes to you; he scolds you, quarrels with you, and even beats you. He is utterly unreasonable in all that he does. You should be very angry with him, but somehow you let everything go without knowing why. Afterward you begin to wonder why it was that when you were scolded you forgot to get angry. After that person did so much, you ought to have lost your temper. If you keep on remembering all that he did to you, you will no doubt be very angry. Yet, to your own amazement, you just unconsciously let everything pass. Let me tell you, victories are all won unawares.

Why is it that you overcome without being conscious of it? It is because a law is working. If it were a matter of your will, you would have to think and hold on. But what the Lord does is to give the victory without your awareness. Such victories are real victories. If you have experienced this even once, then you will understand the revelation that the indwelling Holy Spirit is able to keep you from sin. He is able to make you victorious without the help of your resolves. You do not need to make resolutions, for the law in you will deliver you from sin. If you really see before God that since you are in Christ Jesus, the law of the Spirit of life is also in you, then you will find that the Lord puts His Spirit in you in order to carry you through to victory quite naturally. You do not need to will or to grasp; you will just surprisingly be brought into victory.

To overcome sin does not require an ounce of strength, for it is the work of the law. There is one law which makes me sin without my effort, and there is another law which sets me free from sin—also without my labor. Only that which requires no exertion is true victory. I have nothing to do. Let me tell you, we now have nothing to do but to raise our heads and tell the Lord, "Nothing of me." What happened before was due to law; what is now happening is also due to law. The former law did a thorough work, for it made me sin continuously; this new law does an even better work because I am no longer handicapped by sin. The law of the Spirit of life has manifested itself; it is far superior to the law of sin and death.

If new believers can be brought to see this from the first day of their Christian life, they will then walk the road of deliverance. The Bible never uses the term "overcome sin"; it only uses the phrase "made free" or "delivered from sin." It is said here in Romans, "For the law of the Spirit of life in Christ Jesus made me free from the law of sin and of death." The law of the Spirit of life has pulled me out of the realm of the law of sin and death. The law of sin and death is still present, but I am no longer there for it to work upon. The earth's gravitational force is present, but if things have been removed to heaven, there is no object for it to act upon.

The law of the Spirit of life is in Christ Jesus and I am also now in Christ Jesus; therefore by this law I am made free from the law of sin and of death. "There is therefore now no disabling to them that are in Christ Jesus." The man in Romans 7 is labeled, "disabled." But this disabled person who is so weak and always sins is now, Paul says, no more disabled in Christ Jesus. How? By the law of the Spirit of life in Christ Jesus which has set him free from the law of sin and of death. Therefore, there is no more disabling. Do you see now how this problem of deliverance is completely solved?

The Way of Deliverance and Freedom

The earlier a new believer knows the way of deliverance, the better it is for him. There is no need for a delay of several years before he can know deliverance and freedom. Within a few months he can have many experiences of learning. It is not necessary for him to suffer many wounds before learning. It is possible for a Christian not to be defeated. So, when you are faced with a difficulty, do not strive, using your willpower. If you are defeated, do not turn back. Learn the way of deliverance step by step. The first step is to see that sin is a law to you; the second, to see that the will cannot overcome the law; and the third, to see that there is another law which does overcome the law of sin. Upon experiencing these three steps, the problem is wholly solved.

May all Christians be able to sing the victory song of praise. How many miles are walked unnecessarily; how many tears are shed because of defeat. If believers see this way of deliverance and freedom from the beginning of their Christian lives, they will be saved many sorrows and tears. What is the way of deliverance? It is that the law of the Spirit of life has set me free. It is a law, perfect and powerful. That law is able to deliver me to the end. It does not require my help. As the law of sin in the world causes everybody to sin, so now the law of the Spirit of life in us naturally leads us into complete victory over sin. It naturally makes us holy, full of life, and full of its power.

You have already received life. Never think that the Holy Spirit sometimes manifests life and sometimes not. If this is your case, you do not know the Holy Spirit as a law. Since He is a law, He is always the same. He is the same wherever, whatever, and whenever it may be. He is the same, not because you make Him so, but because He is so. Do you believe He is a law? I have no way to persuade you to believe. If you have not seen this, you will not believe what we have said. May God open your eyes that you may see this. We have in us not only the Holy Spirit, not only life, but also a law. Thus we shall be delivered.

Having seen this law, our problem is resolved. It is not enough to see the indwelling Holy Spirit; we must see Him as a law in us. Then we shall begin to praise. Hereafter, we shall live a transcendent life. How wonderful it is.

OUR LIFE

Christ, our life . . .

Col. 3:4

For to me to live is Christ . . .

Phil. 1:21

I have been crucified with Christ; and it is no longer I that live, but Christ liveth in me: and that life which I now live in the flesh I live in faith, the faith which is in the Son of God, who loved me, and gave himself up for me.

Gal. 2:20

The Relationship Between Christ and Us

What is man's relationship with Christ? It is not, as many seem to think, that we should try to walk in the footsteps of our Lord, imitating, following, and copying Him. True, the Bible does indeed charge us to imitate our Lord, but this is not the only charge in the Bible. Before we can imitate Him, there needs first to be something else. The command to imitate the Lord is not a single, independent command. To try to imitate Him will end up in failure all too often. The Lord is not like a copybook. Should you try to copy Him, you will discover how poorly you write! As a matter of fact, the power of flesh and blood is absolutely incapable of imitating the Lord.

Some may say, is it not written in the Bible that "I can do all things through him [Christ] that strengtheneth me" (Phil. 4:13)? Many Christians realize that they do not have strength, so they ask the Lord to give it to them. Things they should do—commands in the Bible they should keep, examples set by the Lord they should follow—they simply do not have strength for. Therefore, they ask the Lord to give them strength so they can do all things. Daily they wait on the Lord to give them strength so that they may be made able.

Of course, it is right to be strengthened by the Lord; but, apart from this strengthening, something else is necessary. Without this something else, however much we wait on the Lord for power, we will not be given the power we need. Some times our prayers may seem to be answered but other times not. Yet, when the Lord gives power, we can do all things. When power is not given, we cannot even do the first thing in hand. Thus we are often defeated. Yes, we should ask the Lord for power, but we should not take this as a separate, isolated command. Besides the power the Lord gives, there is more He wants to supply us with.

Young brothers and sisters need to thoroughly understand these two things: to imitate the Lord alone is futile, and to depend on the Lord's power only is also ineffective. Notice especially the words, "alone" and "only," for we do not want you to go to extremes. Depending on imitation or strengthening alone, as many older brothers and sisters can testify, leads to failure and defeat.

What, then, according to the Bible should be the relationship between the Lord and us? The principal relationship is that Christ should be our life. Once Christ has become our life, we are able to imitate Him. After He is our life, we may ask Him to give us strength. If we are ignorant of Christ our life, we can never properly copy the Lord nor receive His all-sufficient power. The secret of Christ our life must first be seen and possessed. This order makes all the difference.

If we are ignorant of Christ our life, that to live is Christ, we will not be able to experience the Lord's life on earth. We will neither be able to follow the Lord nor to conquer by His power. Colossians 3 says, "Christ is our life"; Philippians 1 says, "For to me to live is Christ." This alone is the way; this is the victory.

The Secret of Christian Life

Many people greatly misunderstand Colossians 3:4, Philippians 1:21, and Galatians 2:20, especially the latter two. In Philippians 1, Paul tells us that, "For to me to live is Christ." To him, this is a fact. But among God's children today, there is a big misunderstanding. They think, "For to me to live is Christ," is a goal to reach. They must try to so live that they may arrive at the goal. It is a standard to reach; it is their expectation. Let us remember, however, that Paul is not telling us here that his goal is "to me to live is Christ." He is not saying that he must go through many years, trials, and dealings of God before he can reach the goal. What he says is that the reason why he lives is Christ. Without Christ, he cannot live at all. This describes his present condition, not his goal. This is the secret of his life, not his hope. His life is Christ; he lives because Christ lives in him.

Galatians 2:20 is another familiar verse among Christians. The misunderstanding many have with this verse is even graver than with Philippians 1. Again, they take this verse as their goal, as their standard. How they pray and wait and long to arrive at a point where "it is no longer I that live, but Christ liveth in me."

But is Galatians 2:20 a hope? Is it a goal? Is it a standard to arrive at? Many make it so. They hope that one day they will arrive at the place where they no longer live, but Christ lives in them. This is their goal. What they fail to see is that this is God's *way* of victory, not a goal or a standard. It does not say what I should do that I may live; neither does it say what I can do to make me live. It simply says that Christ lives in me.

Galatians 2:20 is not a standard or a goal. It is not something which is set high above man for him to exert his utmost strength to reach. Rather, it is the secret of life.

1. VICTORY THROUGH A SUBSTITUTIONARY LIFE

What is the secret of life? It means that the way of victory is not a goal but a process. Do not confuse the process with the goal. This is a marvelous grace God has given us. It is a way by which the defeated may overcome, the unclean may be clean, the common may become holy, the earthly may be heavenly, and the carnal may become spiritual. It is a way, not a goal. The way lies via a substitutionary life. As Christ is our substitute in death, so is He our substitute in life.

At the beginning of our Christian life, we saw how the

Lord Jesus bore our sins on the cross so that by His death we were delivered from death, our sins were forgiven, and we were condemned no more. Today Paul tells me that because Christ lives in me, I am delivered from living. The meaning here is simple: since He lives in me, I no longer need to live. As He died on the cross for me, so now He lives in me in my place. This is the secret of victory. This is Paul's secret. He does not say, "I hope I will not need to live," or, "I hope I can let Him live." He just says, "No longer live I, for I have let Him live. Now it is no longer I who live, but Christ who lives in me."

Let us pray much that God will enlighten us to see that man has no need to live for himself because Christ can live in him. The day that you heard you did not need to die, you felt this was a great gospel. Now, in another day, you are hearing that you do not need to live. This is also a great gospel.

New believers often have lots of problems. If you instruct them how they ought to maintain a good testimony and live a good Christian life, how they should not love the world but resist temptation, how they must suffer, bear the cross, seek God's will and learn to obey God, they will think that the Christian life is really exhausting. Many of those who have believed in the Lord do feel this way. They toil every day, sighing as they toil. They strive daily but always fail. They try to maintain a testimony, yet they disgrace the Lord all the time. Thus many say they are tired and weary of being Christians. To be a Christian has become a heavy burden.

Many try to resist sin, but do not have the strength. Yet, if they do not resist, they will not have inward peace. Many want to be patient but cannot. When they lose their temper, they feel uneasy in their hearts. They have no

111

heart strength to love; but if they hate, their hearts condemn them. They really feel it is a heavy burden to be a Christian. It gives them the sensation of climbing uphill with a heavy load. Many people will tell you that before they believed in the Lord Jesus, they were heavily laden with the load of sin; now, having believed, they are heavily laden with the burden of holiness. It is only substituting one burden for another; both burdens are tiresome and heavy.

If the situation described above is the case, it certainly means that these Christians have been misinstructed. It is wrong for a person to attempt to live the Christian life. We are not asked to do so. The Word of the Lord says, "It is no longer I that live, but Christ liveth in me." This is the secret of Christian living. The Lord in me lives the Christian life, not I. If I have been trying to live like a Christian, in patience, love, kindness, humility, sorrow or cross-bearing, it is rather painful. But if it is Christ who lives in me, in patience, love, suffering, or cross-bearing, it is joyful.

So, when you find brothers and sisters who are tired of trying to live like a Christian, you should tell them that there is something much better. This will be a great gospel to them. Tell them they have no need to live such a weary life. They need not exhaust themselves to live like Christians; neither do they need to bear a heavy load. As they once thanked God upon hearing the gospel that they had no need to die, now they can thank God as they hear Him say they have no need to live. What a deliverance this is from a tired, exhausted Christian life.

Death is painful, but for us to try to live before God is also painful. How can people such as we, who know nothing about God's holiness, love, the Holy Spirit, or the cross, live in the presence of God? Such a heavy burden is unbearable. The longer we live, the more we sigh. The longer we live, the more frustrated we are. The gospel delivered to you today is that you do not need to live. God has exempted you from living. This, indeed, is a great gospel.

2. NOT I, BUT CHRIST

As it is good news that we need not die, so it is good news that we need not live. For a person to strive to live as a Christian is really an exhausting, impossible task. To ask an impatient, ill-tempered, proud person to live humbly will soon wear him out; he will be worn out by trying to be humble. No wonder the man in Romans 7 was tired! "For to will is present with me, but to do that which is good is not." To daily will to do good, yet daily be unable to do it—how very tiring this is. Then one day the gospel is preached to him, telling him that the Lord does not expect him to do good. Oh, this is a great gospel. The Lord does not require you to do good, neither does He want you to will to do good. He wants to come and live in you. The issue is not whether there is any good, but who does the good.

It is painful for you to try to live before God, for you can never satisfy His demands. You have to confess: "Lord, I knew thee that thou art a hard man, reaping where thou didst not sow, and gathering where thou didst not scatter" (Matt. 25:24). You are totally unable to answer God's requirement.

How, then, are you to live the Christian life? Certainly it is not by taking a carnal, sinful person to heaven and making him a slave. It is indeed fortunate that no carnal person does go to heaven for, were he to do so, he would speedily want to escape. He would not be able to stand it even for one day. How could he endure God's demands? How different his temperament, opinion, way and outlook are from God's. If he were brought to God, he would want to flee away quickly.

Therefore, God's way and His secret for me is not in asking me to imitate the Lord Jesus, nor parceling out power to me in response to my begging that I may be like Christ. God's way for me is what Paul expresses, "No longer I that live, but Christ liveth in me." Do you notice the difference? It is neither a life of imitating Christ nor a life of having power given; rather, it is a substitutionary life. It is no longer you, for God will not allow you to live before Him. It is Christ who lives in you and stands before the presence of God. So, it is not my imitating Christ, not my receiving the power of Christ, but letting Christ live in me.

You have to come to this point of not I, but Christ. This is the believer's life. Formerly I lived but Christ did not; now I do not live but Christ does. If a person cannot say, "Not I, but Christ," he has no knowledge of what Christianity or the Christian life is. It is evident that he is merely hoping to so live that it may be Christ and not him. But Paul tells us it is not this way. He tells us that the way is to let Christ live.

Crucified with Christ

At this point, you will most likely ask, how can I get out of the way so Christ can live? This is indeed a big problem. How can it be, "no longer I"? The answer is found in the first part of Galatians 2:20: "I have been crucified with Christ." Unless I am crucified, I cannot be removed.

Unless I am crucified, it will still be I. It can be no longer I only if I am crucified with Christ.

There are two sides which must be fulfilled before we can have any experience of being crucified with Christ.

First, there is the Lord's work. One needs to have his eyes opened to see that when the Lord Jesus died on the cross, I too was there and was crucified together with Him. I need not again be crucified with Christ. Christ was crucified over nineteen hundred years ago and I with Him. It would not be co-crucifixion if I have to be crucified again some nineteen hundred years later. If I was crucified with Christ, it means I was crucified at the same time Christ was. It means I died when He died. I was hung on His cross; I was with Him. He did not have to come after me. When the Lord Jesus went to the cross, God put me in Christ and thus I died with Him. This is God's work.

Over nineteen hundred years ago, God put my sins on Christ. When I believed on the Lord Jesus who died for me and bore my sins in His body, I cannot say that what He did was done only yesterday. Rather, I say that what He did happened over nineteen hundred years ago. More than nineteen centuries ago, God put my sins on the Lord Jesus who bore them for me. Likewise, when He was crucified, God also put me in Him. Even as my sin problem was solved nineteen hundred years ago, so was the problem of myself solved nineteen hundred years ago. At the time when God put my sins on the Lord Jesus, He also put me in the Lord Jesus. When the Lord died on the cross, I was there and I died too. I was finished there.

Please remember: your sin problem was solved on the cross, and on the same cross you yourself were also finished. We must recall what Romans 6 states, "Knowing this, that our old man was crucified with him" (v. 6). It is not that my old man wishes to be crucified with Him, but that my old man *was* crucified with Him. It is not wishing or hoping. The word in Greek is quite emphatic. It is *"was,"* distinctly indicating that I have once and for all, absolutely and unchangingly, been crucified with Him. Since God put me in Christ, I died when He died on the cross.

By way of illustration, I have a paper here with the words "one hundredth anniversary" written on it. If I tear the paper, I tear these words too. I only tear the paper, I do not tear the words; but in tearing the paper, I also tear the "one hundredth anniversary." Or to use another illustration: the veil in the Bible had cherubim embroidered on it. One day, at the time when the Lord Jesus departed this life, God rent the veil from top to bottom. May I ask, were the cherubim rent when the veil was rent? Surely; when the veil was rent, so were the cherubim rent.

The letter to the Hebrews informs us that the veil points to the flesh of our Lord Jesus (Heb. 10:20). The Bible also shows us that the cherubim represent God's creatures. The faces of the cherubim are the face of a lion, the face of an ox, the face of an eagle, and the face of a man. These stand for God's creatures. Because God put the whole creation in the Lord Jesus, the whole creation was rent when His body was broken. When He died, the old creation passed away. This shows you that God already crucified you with Christ, you who for so many years have tried yourself to live the Christian life. When the Lord Jesus was crucified, you and the whole old creation were rent too. The flesh of our Lord Jesus was rent like a veil and the whole old creation thus passed away.

This is something you must believe. As your eyes were

116

once opened to see your sins laid on Christ, so must your eyes be opened to see your person hid in Christ. Your sins were borne, your person was crucified. This is not your problem, but Christ's, for He has done it for you. Do not look within yourself. Your sins are no longer in you but on the cross. So is your person no longer here but there on the cross. Those who are defeated always look within themselves; those who believe look at the cross. Our sins are there, on the cross, not here; the sinner is also there, not here. We must see that the man is on the cross, not here in us. This is what the Lord has done. It is finished. God has put us in Christ and made us die with Him. Christ has died, we too have died. This is the first side.

But why, then, is it that I am still alive today? I who was crucified am still alive. Here is where your faith comes in. You need to exercise your will and stand on God's side. If you daily expect yourself to be good and to do good, then you are seeing yourself as alive. Your "self" will live again—if he were not alive before. Since you expect him to live, he will live. He cannot die in peace. Many people make such a request of themselves. But you should see what the Lord has done for you. He has crucified you. What is death? It is weakness to the last degree. A person gets weak and becomes weaker and weaker till he reaches the utmost of weakness, that is, death.

Why is Romans 7 in the Bible? Because Romans 7 contradicts Romans 6. In chapter 6, the Lord has crucified us; but in chapter 7, I will to do good. Hence we need to see the two sides. On the one side, I have died in Christ; on the other side, I need to be a crucified person, so that I myself will not be doing things. This second side is my side. I must say: "Lord, I am undone, and I do not believe I am

117

able. Lord, I cannot do good; neither would I do good. Lord, I am evil, but I do not mean to do evil." By not doing, the work is done.

For example, suppose you have no patience. What will you do? Naturally you would like to be patient, you try to be patient, you do your best to be patient, you pray for patience, and you work for patience. However, the more you desire to be patient, the less you are able. The Lord, though, has already crucified the impatient you. What you should say is, "Lord, I cannot be patient. I do not intend to be patient myself. Lord, I am an impatient man. Therefore I will not try to be patient." This is the way to salvation.

The Lord has crucified you and you respond with, "Amen." Since the Lord has crucified you, will you try yourself to be patient? The Lord says, "You are undone; therefore you have been crucified." Yet you answer, "Let me try to be patient; let me try to act as a Christian." But you are asking the wrong person to act as a Christian; you are mistaken. Excuse me for putting it crudely: as neither a cat nor a dog can act like a Christian, neither can you. If you are able to make a cat or a dog be like Christ, then you can make yourself like Him. But we are all very far from God, as far from Him as the lowly animals. I know these are unpleasant words, but this is the situation. The Lord has already decreed that you cannot, that you are only fit to be crucified. But you do not agree. You still want to try, strive, and pray. The Lord says you are undone, so why not confess that you are undone? The Lord says "Die"; why not respond with, "Yes, let me die"? As soon as you say it, you experience it.

What is Romans 7? Romans 7 tells us that the dead man is protesting. The Lord has crucified my old man, yet

I protest. I still make resolutions to do good. It is only after I have failed repeatedly that I acknowledge defeat. Then I finally bow my head and say, "You have not done wrong in crucifying me, for I am really undone." Brothers and sisters, do you see what salvation is? The way of salvation is in accepting the Lord's decision about you. For example: a judge sentences a criminal to death. We know no sinner feels inclined to accept his sentence. Many criminals feel that they do not deserve death because they are still quite good. Rarely do we find one who confesses that he deserves nothing but death, that he is so bad. God's estimate of us is the cross. According to what He sees, we are totally undone. If it were not so, He would not have crucified us. Blessed are we if we can see ourselves as God sees us. We need to be brought to the place where we can accept God's judgment.

Therefore, there are these two sides in our experiencing co-crucifixion. On the one side, Christ has died, so I have been crucified. This is the work of God. On the other side, I must acknowledge this fact and say "Amen" to it. I should not try to remold myself all the time. If I am still making resolutions, trying to be patient and humble, my reaction will counteract the work of Christ and render it ineffective. What I should do is bow my head and say, "You have said I must be crucified; I also say I must be crucified. You have said I am useless; I too say I am useless. You have said I have no patience, so hereafter I will not try to be patient. You have said I cannot be humble; hereafter I will not seek by myself to be humble." Remember, it is the will to be humble that spoils the life. It is the will to be patient that blocks the victory. I am a person who has no patience, so why should I will to be patient? I am a person who has no humility; why should I will to be humble? I deserve nothing but death on the cross.

The Victorious Life

Now I declare that I am a crucified person. If I am to live today, it is no longer I who live but Christ lives in me. I am undone, but Christ has come. This is the way of victory. This is what Paul has shown us. This is how he lives the Christian life. What is the Christian life? Only this—that it is no longer I who live but I let Christ live for me.

I have been wrong all these years: sinful, weak, undone, proud, ill-tempered. But now I come into the presence of the Lord, saying, "Lord, I am undone. Starting from today I wash my hands of my own efforts. Please take over." This is what is meant by "no longer I that live but Christ liveth in me." "I have lived long enough; I am sick of living; now, Lord, will you please try?" Let me tell you, it is as simple as that. The victorious life is none other than this: you need not live. You do not need to exhaust yourself in living; you need only look up and say, "Hereafter I will manage no more; You live and manifest Yourself!" So shall it be done.

Do not consider this very difficult or deep. Remember, new believers should learn this during their first few weeks. They should learn from the first day that they no longer live but Christ lives for them. This is something they must see and a position they must take. The basic problem is that many have not yet given up hope of themselves; they are still trying to make resolutions.

Do you know what is meant by giving up hope? When a person in your home can do nothing right, you no longer say anything to him. He is hopeless. This is what the Lord Jesus has done to you; He has already given you up as hopeless. If He had not done so, He would not have crucified you. If there were any hope, He certainly would not crucify you. The Lord has already given you up as beyond hope, but you are still trying. The more you fall, the quicker you rise. The more you sin, the stronger you resolve. You have not given yourself up. One day, God shows mercy to you, enabling you to see that as God has reckoned you as undone, so you must reckon yourself as undone; since God has judged you to deserve nothing but death, you too judge yourself accordingly. Then it will be quite easy for you to come to the Lord and say, "I was crucified with Christ; I no longer live. Not only You have crucified me, but I also have no intention to live. Henceforth, it is no longer I, but You who live."

Hereafter, you take a positive course. As you deal with the Lord, you tell Him, "Lord, I accept You to be my life. Hereafter, I acknowledge Christ as my life. I confess that to me to live is Christ." This will become your daily life before God, trusting in the Lord. "Lord, this is Your business, not mine." Your temptation is not to sin; rather, your temptation is to act on your own.

I have said this for many years, and I will say it again: the basic aim of temptation is not so much to get us to sin as to get our old man to act. Temptation lies in tempting our old man to resist. If the old man can rise up to resist temptation, he can also rise up to commit sin. So whenever temptation comes, we must refuse to move. "Lord, this is Your business, not mine. Lord, I look to You, for You live for me." It is thus you learn to trust the Lord to live in you.

You need to believe daily; you should tell the Lord specifically, "Lord, I am useless. I accept your cross. Lord,

keep me so that I make no move. Under every circumstance, Lord, You take the initiative. Lord, You are the
Lord and so You live." Let me tell you, if you thus look to
the Lord and trust Him daily, you will also be able to
daily testify that it is indeed no longer you who lives but
Christ who lives in you.

"And that life which I now live in the flesh I live in
faith, the faith which is in the Son of God." What does
Christ living in me mean? It simply means that hereafter I
live in the faith of the Son of God. I daily believe that the
Son of God lives in me. "Lord, I believe You live for me.
Lord, I believe You are my life, and I believe that You live
in me." As I thus believe and so live, I will no longer make
any move no matter what happens. If one has not learned
well the basic teaching of Romans 7, he is a useless person.
The basic lesson there is that one should not make
resolutions. In other words, its basic lesson is to see the
futility of making resolutions and thus to quit making
them. If resistance is useless, hereafter I will not resist. If
my action is vain, henceforth I will not move. I will tell the
Lord, "Lord, hereafter I will not do it again. I am
finished."

Learn to look up, not to do something. We are saved by
faith, not by works, and our life is of faith, not of works.
We are saved by looking up to the Lord, and so shall we
live in the same way. Let us look up and say, "It is You,
not I." As in initial salvation it was not anything I did but
what the Lord did, so today I live on earth not by myself
but by the Lord. Learn to believe in the Son of God. Say to
the Lord, "Lord, You are the One whom I believe.
Everything depends on You. I would that You live in me."

I do not insist that you say these words. But I do ask, do
you have this foundation? Brethren, are you clear about

this? Defeat is not caused by less work but by too much of the work of man. When we are working, God's grace cannot come to us, and so our sins are not forgiven. Likewise, in our much working, the life of the Lord cannot be manifested. This is a principle to be remembered.

The efficacy of the cross can never be manifested in those who trust in their works. If I always try to do good, I will not be saved. But when I cease trusting myself and look up to the Lord, then I am saved. It is the same today. If the cross has not worked in me, I will be working all the time. In such a condition, for me to say, "Not I, but Christ," would be empty. I must learn to condemn myself. I am such a completely hopeless person that I neither try nor pray. I am just quiet. On this sure foundation, I raise my head and say, "Lord, I trust You to live in me. I trust You to be humble for me. I trust You to overcome for me. I trust You to manifest Your life. You are to live my whole life for me." Let me tell you, what you say, the Lord will do for you. If your conduct contradicts your faith, you cannot expect the Lord to do anything for you. This is something you must settle thoroughly.

As soon as a person believes in the Lord, he should start to let Christ live in him. He will immediately experience Christ as his life and he will always be afraid of his own actions. What Romans 7 reveals is the activity of the dead. The man is already dead, yet he still wants to be active. Consequently, he destroys the work of God. Let us therefore learn to live before God—make no move by ourselves, but only move in obedience to the Lord. At that moment, we can really believe. Unless the foundation is right, the Christian life will always be weak. So new believers must be helped to this proper foundation.

THE WILL OF GOD

The Importance of Knowing God's Will

What we will now consider is how a new believer can know the will of God. This is of great importance, for the lack of such knowledge causes great damage to His service.

Before one became a Christian, he lived in the lusts of his flesh, doing the desires of the flesh and of the mind. By nature, he was a child of wrath. Because he served only himself, he tried to please his own self in all things. He would do whatever made him happy. But after he believes in the Lord, he acknowledges Jesus of Nazareth as his Lord whom he will serve. Because he is redeemed, he no longer belongs to himself. He confesses that, having been bought with a price, he is the Lord's and to Him he will render his service.

Because of this, from the day he is saved a child of God undergoes a drastic change in his life. Formerly he felt frustrated if he could not do as he wanted but happy if he could do according to his desire. Such happiness was derived from his own will. But now, his center is changed, for he has a Lord. If he still lives according to his own will, as before, he will not be satisfied; on the contrary, he will feel most uncomfortable.

After you are saved, you discover that the cause of your discomfort lies in following your own will. The more you do things according to your desire, the less happy you are. But if instead of following your own thought you learn to follow God by the new life in you, you will have peace and joy. This, indeed, is a wonderful change. To do God's will is joyful. Never for a moment think that following your own will will make you happy. The way to happiness is not in following your will but in following the will of God.

The life we have received has a primary demand: we should walk according to God's will. The more we do God's will, the happier we are. The less we walk in our own way, the straighter our path before God is. If we do not live according to our own mind, we will have a more ascendant life in God's presence. But if we follow our own will, the going will get harder. Happiness is found in obedience, not in self-will.

This is something which should be shown to new believers. When we believe in the Lord, we go through a change at the very core of our being. The first question we now ask is, "What shall I do, Lord?" Paul asked this question; we too ask. Whenever we meet a problem, we should humble ourselves under the hand of God, saying, "Not according to my will, but according to Your will."

No matter how difficult the circumstance or trial, we are to learn obedience by saying, "Lord, not my will, but Your will." In deciding our future or in choosing our way, we must lay it before the Lord and say, "Lord, not my will, but Your will be done."

Brethren, as soon as you become a Christian, you should

start to accept God's thought. His will alone should govern everything. No one should live according to his own idea. You will be saved many unnecessary wanderings if you are soft and tender before God and learn from the start to submit to His will. The reason many fail in their Christian lives is because they follow their own wills. Remember, to walk according to your own will will give you nothing but sorrow and spiritual poverty. Eventually God will still bring you around to following His will, but He will have to get your submission through special circumstances or unusual dealings. If you were not His child, He could let you go. But since you are His child, He will in His own way steer you onto the road of obedience. All your disobedience will merely cause you to wander unnecessarily. In the end, you will yet obey.

How to Know the Will of God

How can we know God's will? So often we make mistakes. It is not easy for us earth people to understand God's will. However, we have one comfort before God: it is not only that we desire to do God's will, but also God Himself wants us to do it.

We seek to understand His will, and He calls us to know it. Since He wants us to do His will, surely He will enable us to understand. Therefore, it is God's business to reveal His will to us. No child of God need worry about how can he do God's will when he has no knowledge of it. Although it is quite difficult to know God's will, to worry about it is unnecessary. Somehow, God *will* make His will known to us.

Let us learn to believe that since God wants us to do His will He will surely make it known to us. He will use appropriate means to show us what it is. The responsibility of the Master is to make His will known to the servants; the servants are then to obey. If our attitude and intention are that of obedience, we shall see that the Lord will be responsible to tell us His will. Were it not so, then He would be responsible if we did anything wrong. So young believers should learn to trust God to reveal His will to them.

By what means can you know the will of God? There are three things to which you must pay attention. When these three factors fit together, you can be rather sure of what the will of God is. But if these three do not line up, if one of them does not harmonize with the others, then you know you have to wait further before God.

What are these three factors? The first is environmental arrangement; the second, inner sensing of the guidance of the Holy Spirit; and the third, scriptural teaching. Of course, this does not mean that they must be in this order; it simply means that all three are necessary and that when they agree and give the same testimony, then you know the will of God. Whenever one of the three does not agree with the others, you know you must not be hasty but should wait. The point requiring your care is to not be hasty nor try to force anything. Take action only after these three factors dovetail.

1. Environmental Arrangement

Let us look at the factor of environment first. The Bible tells us, "Are not two sparrows sold for a penny?" (Matt. 10:29). In another place, it says, "Are not five sparrows sold for two pence?" (Lk. 12:6). Mathematically, if one penny buys two sparrows, then two pence would buy four sparrows. But the Lord says, two pence will buy five sparrows. This shows how cheap sparrows were. One penny for two, two pence for five, the extra one being added without cost. Yet not even this fifth sparrow could fall to the ground apart from the will of God.

I do not wish to speak of the first or second sparrow, but of the fifth one. Unless it is God's will, this fifth sparrow will not fall to the ground—though it was bought without price, simply being added to the purchase. Thus, the Bible indicates to us that all environmental arrangements, all things which happen in the environment, are expressions of the will of God. No one shall fall to the ground outside of the will of the heavenly Father. Hence, if you see a sparrow on the ground you have met with the will of God.

Let us use human hair as an illustration. Africans have at least an aggregate of eighty to ninety thousand hairs; Chinese have at most a hundred to a hundred and ten thousand; those with light hair have an aggregate of a hundred and twenty thousand hairs. The range therefore is from eighty thousand to a hundred and twenty thousand. Each day many hairs fall and many hairs grow upon our heads. Some believe that our hair changes completely every few years. Yet our Lord says, "Thou canst not make one hair white or black" (Matt. 5:36) without the Father's will. He also says, "But the very hairs of your head are all numbered" (Matt. 10:30). No one knows how many hairs he has. Who has ever counted his hairs? But God has; He has numbered all of them. No person can make his hair naturally white or black; it takes the will of God to make such a change.

New believers ought to learn to know God's will through their environment. There is nothing in our lives that is accidental. Every day's happenings are measured by the Lord. We need to see that everything in our lives—events,

families, husbands, wives, children, schoolmates, relatives
—everything is arranged for us by the Lord. Things which
befall us daily are all within the Father's ordering. We
must learn to know God's will in the environment. This is
the first factor.

Many new believers have not yet learned how to be led
of the Holy Spirit; they may know very little of the
teaching of the Bible. God, though, is still able to guide
them, for they can at least see the hand of God in their
environment. This is the very first step.

"Be ye not as the horse, or as the mule, which have not
understanding; whose trappings must be bit and bridle
to hold them in, else they will not come near unto thee"
(Ps. 32:9). It sometimes seems as if God has to hold us with
bit and bridle, or else we will go astray. We are as ignorant
as the horse and the mule which need to be held by the
outward restraint of bit and bridle. As new believers we
may pray in this manner, "Lord, I am an ignorant mule."
Even older brothers and sisters may also pray, "Lord, I am
but a horse or a mule, without understanding. I am not too
clear on Your Word or on Your guidance. Please hold me
with bit and bridle and do not allow me to go astray."

Trust yourself to the Lord that He will lead you into
obedience by placing you in a particular environment. He
is able to do this. Have you ever seen how the duck farmer
uses a long staff to drive his ducks? He uses a staff more
than twenty feet long. With this staff he keeps the ducks on
the right course. When the ducks go to one side, he beats
them back. Likewise, you can commit yourself to the Lord
saying, "Lord, I am a horse, I am a mule with no
understanding. But I do not want to go astray. How good
it would be if I knew Your will. But since I do not, will
You please hold me with bit and bridle? I am so void of

understanding that I will run away if You loose the bit and bridle. I ask You to encircle me, to drive me to Your will. If I want to run away, I pray You will interfere. Though I know nothing, I do know pain. So please interfere when I do not want Your will."

Do not neglect the arrangement of environment. We need to commit ourselves to the environmental arrangement of the Lord. Although we are like a horse or a mule, with no understanding, inglorious, nevertheless, our being restrained by God is something of exceeding glory.

I do not know what your experience is, but I often feel that a very big problem with many new brothers and sisters is their constant striving against environment. They will not submit; rather, they fight to free themselves from their present circumstances. Such people cannot but be wounded. If they learned to submit to the environment, their path would be much straighter. So do learn to know that the Lord's arrangement in your environment is right. Do not resist what the Lord has done in this respect.

2. GUIDANCE OF THE HOLY SPIRIT

We have seen how the hand of God is manifested in our environment. God does not want us to be like the horse or the mule which has no understanding. He will give us guidance from within. "For as many as are led by the Spirit of God, these are sons of God" (Rom. 8:14). Who can be led by the Spirit of God? The sons of God can, for the Holy Spirit leads us from within. God will not only guide us through environment but also will lead us by His life in our spirit. Remember, we are indwelt by the Holy Spirit; we do have Him in us. Because of this, God can make His will known to us in the deepest part of our beings.

What is the guidance of the Holy Spirit? The prophet Ezekiel tells us that when we are born anew, God gives us a new spirit. "And I will put a new spirit within you" (Ez. 11:19). He further shows us, "And I will put my Spirit within you" (Ez. 36:26–27). We need to distinguish between these two. Does God put His Spirit in us when we are born anew? No, He first gives us a new spirit, and then He gives His Spirit to us. The "new spirit" is man's spirit while "my Spirit" is God's Spirit. So at the time of new birth, God creates in us a new spirit, the human spirit, and then He puts His Spirit within us. Our spirit is like a temple, a house for the Spirit of God to dwell in.

Before we have the new spirit within us, God is unable to give us His Spirit. Were He to do so, His Spirit would not find a dwelling place. During the deluge, the earth was filled with water. God's judgment was upon the whole old creation. When the dove was set free from the ark, she could find no rest for the sole of her foot. It was not until the waters receded, the judgment passed, the old creation perished, and the new creation came in with the new olive-leaves that the dove, again sent forth, found a place to stay. So it is with the Spirit of God. Through the centuries, God has been most willing to give His Spirit to us. However, man's spirit is not only defiled and full of sin, but is also dead. Man's spirit belongs to the old creation; its communication with God has been cut. Consequently, there is absolutely no possibility for His Spirit to dwell in man even if He wants to. For the Spirit of God to dwell in man, the man must be born anew. He needs to have a new spirit within him to provide an abode for the Spirit of God to indwell.

New believers, you have a new spirit, and the Spirit of God also dwells in you. That indwelling Spirit of God will tell you what God's will is. The witness is within you. This is a characteristic of today's believer: he not only knows through environment but also from within. He not only can see the Lord's arrangement in his environment but also the Lord Himself reveals within what His will is. Learn, then, to trust in the guidance of the Holy Spirit within you as well as in God's arrangement of your environment. At the most appropriate moment, the time of need, the Spirit of God within you will not be dumb but will enlighten you and show you whether or not the matter is of God.

As soon as one believes in the Lord, he is able to be led by the Holy Spirit. He need not wait for some future time.

You may remember the story about "The Resident Boss." One year I was recuperating in Kuling Mountain and brother Yu was saved. Not long after he was saved, I departed. This brother drank heavily before he believed in the Lord. He especially would drink more of his home-made wine during the cold Kuling winter. Now both he and his wife were saved. He hardly knew the Chinese characters, hence he could not read the Bible very well. One day he prepared some food and warmed the wine as he had always done in the past. Before he drank, he asked the blessing. Then he asked his wife whether a Christian could drink wine. His wife answered that she did not know. He then said it was a pity that Mr. Nee had already left; otherwise he could ask him. The wife suggested that since the dishes and the wine were ready, why not drink first and afterward write a letter to ask Mr. Nee.

So he blessed the food again. Still he did not feel right. Being Christians, they felt they had to know right then if Christians could drink wine. He asked his wife to take out the Bible, for I had given him a Bible with large print after he was saved. He took a look and was frightened at the thickness of the Bible. He thought it was really a pity that he had not thought to ask Mr. Nee about drinking wine while he was still with them on the mountain.

Later on, I met him again. I asked him what he had done that day. He said, "I did not drink the wine. You were not here, and I did not understand the Bible. But after having blessed the food three times and thought that now I could drink, the Resident Boss within me would not permit me to drink. So, I did not drink."

This story illustrates that if anyone really has the heart to know God's will, he shall know it. Only the careless believer is never clear. If a believer means to do God's will, the Resident Boss will surely tell him. You see, this is Christianity. Not only is there environmental arrangement, but also there is the teaching of the Resident Boss.

In order to know God's will, you need to know something of this inner feeling. However, you should not overemphasize it lest you fall into analysis. What you should see is simply that God's Spirit dwells in the innermost recess of man, that is, in his spirit. That is why the consciousness of the Holy Spirit cannot be shallow or external; it comes from the depth of your being. It does not sound like a voice, and yet it is like a voice. It is not exactly like a feeling, and yet it is like a feeling. The Spirit of the Lord within you will tell you what is His will and what is not His will. If you are the Lord's, when you follow the movement of this life, you have the sense of being right. But if you rebel a little or resist, you feel upset and uncomfortable within you.

Obedience is life to the believer. Do not do anything about which you do not feel peaceful in heart. Whenever you are not at peace, you know the Holy Spirit within you has been displeased. How can the Holy Spirit in you be grieved and you still be joyful? If something is of the Lord, you can undertake it with peace in your heart. If it is not of the Lord, you will not have peace within. The more you do it, the less at peace you are and the less assurance you have. That which is the Lord's leading will naturally give you peace and life. However, you should not analyze your inner feeling too much.

During the past twenty years, I have received enough letters and met enough people to certify how often Christians try to examine their inner feelings. After they are told of the separation of spirit and soul, they start to analyze themselves day in and day out. They inwardly become a laboratory where they unceasingly analyze what is right and what is not right. This is most unhealthy and is a symptom of sickness. We should not allow God's children to do that.

Because one is a child of God, he will know what the feeling in the spirit is. If he knows that something comes from the spirit, that is enough. Should he enter into analysis of his feelings, he must be led away. We hope that God's children will avoid that hardship. Do not analyze your feelings all the time. The only time you need to do that is when there is not enough light. If the light is sufficient, there is no need for analysis. You will know right away. By the Spirit of God within you, you will be clear on all things. If you will to obey God, you will know within you what His will is.

3. SCRIPTURAL TEACHING

The will of God is not only manifested in environment and by His indwelling Holy Spirit, it is also made known to us through the Bible. His will has been revealed many times in the past, and this is recorded in the Holy Scripture. God's will is one will, not two or ten or a hundred or even a thousand wills. God's will is one. He does not change today from yesterday. His will remains the same forever. For this reason, God's children must know the Bible. In it they will find the revelation of God's will.

The way which God views a thing today is the same as He viewed it in the past. What He condemned before, He condemns now. That which He delighted in before is still His delight today. The Bible is the place where God reveals His mind. God manifested His own will concerning many people and many things in the former days. All these are recorded in the Bible. Since God's will is uniform, there are already a number of examples written in the Bible to show us what it is. It is absolutely impossible for God to condemn something today which He has approved in the Bible. Likewise, the Holy Spirit today will never lead us to do that which God already denounced in the Bible. The will of God is one.

The Bible reveals the will of God in a most comprehensive way. It is not a book telling only about a few lives or touching upon just two or three items. No, the Bible is most comprehensive; it covers everything. For a person to know God's will, he must look into the Bible. He must be like a judge who looks into the many court decisions of the past in order to reach the present decision. The court decision of today is based on the laws of yesterday. God's will has already been revealed in the Bible. By looking into the decisions in His Word concerning different matters, you know what God is after today. God does not change His mind now and then. In Christ it is all yea and amen. If God decides on anything, He will carry it out to the end.

Therefore, in order to know God's will, at the very least you have the most trustworthy Word of God before you. In many matters you will be able to know God's will just by reading His Word. God will never do things differently today from what He did in the Bible. There can be increase but never contradiction. God's will is one. For a new believer to know the things of God, he needs to read the Word of God much. Since he may never have read God's Word before he became a Christian, he ought to read it carefully now so that he may learn to know God and His will.

GOD'S WILL KNOWN IN THE AGREEMENT OF THESE THREE FACTORS

These three factors together manifest the will of God— environment, man's spirit, and the Bible. By the agreement of these three we learn to know the will of God. What should we do if we desire to seek God's will in a particular matter? For us to be sure, these three factors must agree. It cannot be just one factor but, rather, the agreement of all three. Then we can be clear of His will.

Suppose someone asks you to go into business or work or travel with him. Or suppose you yourself have the thought of doing something or of entering into a special relationship with certain people. Or suppose someone persuades you to change the course of your future. When you are faced with such decisions, how are you going to know the will of God? According to the principles you have learned here, you first need to go to the Lord and see what the Bible teaches on the matter. Does God have anything to say in His Word on this particular matter? Search the Word to see. That which agrees with the Bible is the Lord's will. Then ask, "How do I inwardly feel? How is the Lord leading me?" Do you feel right within you? You will discover that what the Lord shows you inwardly is the same as what the Bible records openly. If your inner leading does not agree with the Bible, you know the former is untrustworthy. You must further wait and seek. Only when your inner guidance and the Bible agree, do you know that all is well.

When these two agree, then lift your head and say to the Lord, "Oh, Lord, You always manifest Your will in environment. It is absolutely impossible for You to inwardly lead me and outwardly teach me with Your Word and not also have the environment give similar indication. Lord, will You so arrange the environment that it may line up with the Bible and the guidance of the Holy Spirit?" Then you will see that God does indeed manifest His will through environment. Were it not His will, not one hair could turn black or white, nor could a sparrow fall to the ground.

4. The Principle of the Church

God has shown us that His will is manifested in His Word, in man's spirit, and in environment. Now we will add one more factor: God's will is manifested through the church. There is no guidance which can stand independently. God's children today are quite different from His people in the Old Testament. During that time, they became the people of God individually; but today we are God's people corporately. They became God's people as a nation, while we are the people of God as a body.

No hand can move without getting other parts of the

body involved. How can the hand move without the body being moved? How can the eyes see and the body not see? Can the ears hear and the body not hear? The hearing of the ears is the hearing of the body; the seeing of the eyes is the seeing of the body. Although the feet do the walking, the body has walked. Likewise, all of God's guidance is corporate, non-personal, involving the whole body. The light of God is in the holy sanctuary; the glory of God is also there. Whenever the church of God is like a sanctuary, God's glory is manifested there, for the glory of God is in the sanctuary. It is not only that we are individually led of God, but also that the whole body of brothers and sisters receives the Lord's guidance. It is not one person who makes a decision; rather it is the body which decides. We must learn to know God's will by the principle of fellowship.

When these four factors stand in a straight line, all is well. God's will is manifested in environment, in the guidance of the Holy Spirit, in the Bible, and through the church. After one has examined the first three factors, he still needs to consult the church. God tells His will not just to one person but to a body, that is, to all the brothers and sisters. So it is important to be clear in one's inward feeling, in the Word of God, in the environment, and finally in the consent of the church.

If I were the only saved person in the world, then it would be quite sufficient for me alone to be clear of God's will. But there are many saved people in the world, and the Lord says that He dwells in their midst. The principle of Matthew 18 is that I must listen to the church. In that passage there is a brother who has offended another brother. The offending brother has to be told of his offense. Is it not strange that he needs to be told? He has no sensitivity about it as does the other brother. Being a Christian, he ought to be the first to be conscious of his sin. Instead he needs to be reprimanded. He is told that he has sinned against another brother, but he is totally unaware of it. His feeling strives against another's feeling.

When the brother who was offended consults with a few other brothers, they all feel that the first brother has sinned. So they all come to him and tell him he is wrong. Suppose he still honestly feels that he is not wrong. Sometimes people are dishonestly in the dark, but this brother is honestly in the dark. What, then, shall be done? The matter should be told to the church. If all the brothers and sisters judge the offending brother to be wrong, though he himself still does not realize it, the Lord says that he should be looked upon as a Gentile and a publican.

Do you see what guidance is? Guidance means you see the church. This is marvelous. Never believe you are right and the whole body is wrong. You must learn to accept the judgment of the church. When all the brothers and sisters agree in their feeling, you should be careful to accept that feeling of the church. This is a scriptural principle. God's will is manifested in the church. For this reason, the Lord Jesus says, "What things soever ye shall bind on earth shall be bound in heaven; and what things soever ye shall loose on earth shall be loosed in heaven" (Matt. 18:18). The church is where God's light dwells. The church is God's dwelling place. The judgment of the church is the judgment of the Lord.

ASSURANCE COMES FROM THE AGREEMENT OF THESE FOUR FACTORS

The church must learn to walk in God's light. Her responsibility is tremendous. If she acts carelessly in the flesh instead of serving God in the spirit, her judgment will not be dependable. The church must be spiritual, and the brothers and sisters must be subject to authority. Then the will of God will be manifested through these four factors. To know God's will, you should be clear about the teaching of the Bible, clear in your inner leading, clear in God's environmental arrangement, and also clear as to the thought of the church. When these four completely agree, you have a straight path before you. You are assured of the will of God.

The Greatness of Knowing God's Will

Many seem to think that knowing God's will is a small thing. But let me tell you, for us who are but as small insects to know the will of God is, indeed, a big thing. For many years I have thought how marvelous it is that we who are like insects and worms, can claim to know God's will. Truly we are but worms; yet we do know God's decisions. Is this not a big thing, something worthy to boast of? May new believers realize that it is glorious to know the will of God. Having walked this way for over twenty years, we do know something of the greatness of knowing God's will. God condescends Himself to make His will known to us. We need to bow and worship and treasure this knowledge.

The Problem of Man

Finally, though all the preceding four factors seem to give a positive indication, it still does not necessarily guarantee that one has found the will of God, for he who trusts in methods may not be right. He needs to cry from the bottom of his heart, "Lord, I am Your servant; I will do Your will."

In the Old Testament there was a rule for the slave who wished to serve his master forever. He would have an awl thrust through his ear unto the door (Deut. 15:15). From a human standpoint, this may seem cruel, but the Lord shows us that it is what we ought to do. We should come to the Lord and say, "My ear is pierced through to the door. It is opened to hear Your word. I will serve You, and I will gladly do Your will. From my heart I beg that I may serve You, for You are my Master. I have a strong desire to be Your servant. Let me hear Your word and know Your will." We must come to the Lord and ask to hear His word. Our ears are pierced so that we hearken to His word. We wait for the Lord's command; we wait to be sent.

I am often troubled that many seek to know how to know God's will without really having the heart to do it. They want to know the proper method. They seem to look upon God's will as a kind of knowledge to be stored away unused. They consult with God to know His will, but then they confer with their own thoughts. Do not forget the word of the Lord Jesus, "If any man willeth to do his will, he shall know" (John 7:17). Let us really desire to know God's will. Let us take God's will as our food and our life. Let us learn to obey His will.

If both the man and the method are right, it is useful. But if the man is not right, there is no effectiveness in the method. What I fear most is people wanting to know the method of how to know God's will while being themselves rebellious before Him. May I remind you that the Christian way is a transcendent way. If you have a warm and perfect heart toward God, willing to do His will, then you will know it even though you are totally ignorant of methods. God will make His will known to those who know nothing of methods. It is a wonderful thing that the eyes of the Lord run to and fro throughout the whole earth (2 Chron. 16:9). The words, "to and fro," in Hebrew carry the idea of looking again as if the first look were not quite adequate. The eyes of the Lord look to and fro to find if there is anyone who seeks after His will. To such a one, God shall manifest Himself.

Today with a heart perfect toward the Lord you may say, "Lord, I really want Your will." Let me tell you, even if you know nothing of the methods of knowing God's will, you still will know it. God must show you His will. He must reveal His heart to you. He may even use the lightning in the sky to communicate His mind to you. No believer needs to wait for years before he comes to know God's will. We wish all believers would present their all to God from the very first day. Rather that they should offer their hearts than that the Christian standard be lowered.

TITLES YOU
WILL WANT TO HAVE

by Watchman Nee

ORDER FROM:

Christian Fellowship Publishers, Inc.
11515 Allecingie Parkway
Richmond, Virginia 23235